Wildflowers
of the Blue Ridge Parkway

D0907873

Wildflowers

of the Blue Ridge Parkway

J. Anthony Alderman

The University of

North Carolina Press

Chapel Hill and London

© 1997

The University of North Carolina Press

All rights reserved

Manufactured in the United States of America

The paper in this book meets the guidelines for
permanence and durability of the Committee on
Production Guidelines for Book Longevity of
the Council on Library Resources.

This book was set in Monotype Garamond
by Eric M. Brooks.

Book design by Richard Hendel.

Library of Congress
Cataloging-in-Publication Data
Alderman, J. Anthony (John Anthony)
Wildflowers of the Blue Ridge Parkway /
J. Anthony Alderman.
p. cm.
Includes bibliographical references (p.   )
and index.
ISBN 0-8078-4651-1 (pbk.: alk. paper)
1. Wild flowers—Blue Ridge Parkway (N.C. and
Va.)—Identification.   2. Blue Ridge Parkway
(N.C. and Va.)   I. Title.
QK122.3.A53   1997   96-47698
582.13'097568—dc21   CIP

01 00 99 98 97   5 4 3 2 1

To the memory of my mother,

Irene Cureton Alderman.

With love and patience, she opened

my eyes to the wonders of nature.

Contents

Acknowledgments

I express my appreciation to my family and friends, whose continued words of encouragement helped make this book possible. My thanks also to the National Park Service and the rangers who assisted me and watched over me during my fieldwork along the Parkway. My special thanks to Rangers Terry Morris and Janet Bachman for their many kindnesses and assistance in locating several elusive species. Special thanks also to Dr. George Nester and Naturalist Janette Lawler of Explore Park and to Steve Miller and Parker Flowers, who furnished the wildflower inventory for Grandfather Mountain.

Introduction

This book will be your traveling companion as you explore the wildflowers of the Blue Ridge Parkway. It comes to you as the result of a lifelong love affair with nature, the seeds of which were planted over half a century ago when my mother, with love and great patience, opened my eyes to the beauty and wonders of the natural world. At about that same time, on September 11, 1935, far from my south Texas home, ground was being broken for a paved road to run along the crest of the Blue Ridge Mountains, connecting the Shenandoah and the Great Smoky Mountains national parks.

The huge gap between these two seemingly unrelated events began to narrow during the autumn of 1987. On September 11 of that year, the ceremonial opening of the Linn Cove Viaduct signaled completion of the final section of the Blue Ridge Parkway. On that same day, just a short distance away, I stood on a Parkway overlook observing the annual fall migration of the birds of prey. It was the migration of hawks that lured me to the Parkway that warm fall day, but it was the magnetism of the luxuriant and diverse mountain wildflowers that kept drawing me back long after the hawks were gone.

The Blue Ridge Parkway is a jewel in our nation's system of national parks. Coursing along the backbone of the southern Appalachian Mountains, considered among the oldest mountain ranges in the world, the Parkway provides endless, breathtaking views of distant ridges, lush valleys, creeks and rivers, villages and towns. Beginning at Mile 0, near Waynesboro, Virginia, where the Shenandoah National Park's Skyline Drive ends, the Parkway winds and twists its way along the crests of the Blue Ridge Mountains for its first 355 miles. For the remaining 114 miles of its length, it skirts the southern tip of the massive Black Mountains and snakes its way through the Craggies, the Pisgahs, and the Balsams before coming to an end at the Great Smoky Mountains National Park near Cherokee, North Carolina, just a stone's throw from the Tennessee–North Carolina border.

As its builders intended, the Blue Ridge Parkway provides a leisurely paced tour through a land of rugged mountain beauty for millions of visitors annually. A trip along the Parkway is like a slow-motion, roller-coaster journey through times long past. The mountains provide a quiet refuge of natural beauty, with forested ridges, rural landscapes, weathered cabins, split-rail fences, a delightful array of wild creatures, and a continually changing spectrum of wildflowers.

The Parkway is mostly an up-and-down road, its constant and drastic changes in elevation ranging from a low of 649 feet above sea level at the James River Visitor Center and Museum at Mile 63.6 in Virginia, to a high of 6,047 feet at the Richland–Balsam Overlook, at Mile 431.4 in North Carolina. Forty-three peaks along or within view of the Parkway rise above 6,000 feet, and one, Mount Mitchell, soaring to 6,684 feet, is the highest peak east of the Mississippi River. Old-timers in these parts say the mountains are so high that one has to "lie down and look up to see out."

This wide range of elevations means that the Parkway cuts across several climatic zones. It is said, in fact, that a trip from the Parkway's northern foothills to the higher southern elevations transcends as many different plant life zones as would be encountered during a 1,000-mile trip from central Georgia to central Quebec. This results, of course, in profound changes in atmospheric conditions, including moisture and temperature.

Mountain air is relatively cool, and this element probably strikes a visitor almost as much as the height and massiveness of the terrain. In fact, average temperatures drop about 3 degrees for every 1,000-foot increase in elevation, with some of the highest elevations recording average temperatures 10 to 20 degrees cooler than the lowest elevations. This results in frost-free seasons of about 100 days at the higher elevations and close to 200 days at the lower elevations.

Differences in elevation also have a significant effect on rainfall. Upper elevations, often shrouded in the blue haze for which these mountains are famous, record average annual rainfalls of as much as 80 inches, while lower elevations get closer to 50 inches.

These variations in temperature and moisture result in a diversity in plant life that is one of the most distinctive features of the southern Appalachian Mountains. Slightly more than 300 species of flowering plants are indigenous to the Parkway's mountains, and nearly 350 more are shared by the mountains and the Piedmont regions to the east. It is not surprising that this region attracted the attention of botanists at an early date.

Perhaps the first botanist to study the plant life of these mountains was the American William Bartram, who came to the Blue Ridge in 1776 and published a record of his travels in 1791. He was followed by André Michaux, a Frenchman who visited the region first in 1776 and returned in 1802 with an appointment from the French government to collect plants for the royal gardens. It is said that Michaux collected 2,500 plants, shrubs, and trees from western North Carolina. One of the Parkway's most interesting wildflowers, the Michaux saxifrage with its tiny white, yellow-spotted flowers, was named in his honor.

John Fraser, a Scotsman, studied the mountain flora of the Blue Ridge between 1787 and 1799 under sponsorship of the Russian government. American Asa Gray explored the area in 1841 and reported encountering a greater number of indigenous trees during a trip through western North Carolina than he did during a trip through Europe. Gray's *Manual of Botany*, first published in 1848, was the first accurate and modern guide to the plants of eastern North America. Even to this day, *Gray's Manual* is still widely used by students of botany. One of the mountains' rarest wildflowers, the Gray's lily, was named in his honor.

Undoubtedly, the most noted of the botanists who studied the mountain flora was an Englishman named John Lyon, who followed in the footsteps of André Michaux, studying and collecting the plants of the southern Appalachians from 1799 until his death in 1814. The Lyon's turtlehead (*Chelone lyonii*) was named in his honor, as was a genus of shrubs that include the male blueberry (*Lyonia ligustrina*).

What the early botanists discovered many years ago is no less true today. The relationship of plants to their environment is nowhere more complex than here in these mountains. Within a short distance, each slope may display variations in temperature, moisture, wind, soil, and amount of sunlight. Among these conditions each plant settles where it is best suited and adapts itself to survival.

Most of the plants along the Parkway are native plants, that is, they are indigenous to the area in which they are found. Some however, are alien species brought to this country, usually as ornamentals, from other parts of the world. Many of the alien plants escaped cultivation, found a suitable niche in the wild, and now thrive there alongside the native species.

It has long been recognized that human activity along the mountain ridges has had a profound effect on plant life. Many of the wildflowers that are so-called weeds thrive in disturbed areas, and humans have done a good job of disturbing the natural landscape. Plant habitats have been altered by homesites, farms, roads, and commercial ventures. Even along the Parkway itself, mowing operations discourage the growth of some plants but encourage the growth of others. In all fairness to humans, however, it must be noted that nature too has had a hand in changing the landscape. Windstorms, landslides, floods, and lightning-ignited fires do much to destroy habitats and create new ones.

Because of the diverse habitats they harbor and thanks to the propagation of seeds by birds, animals, insects, and wind, the mountains of the Blue Ridge play host to an unusual abundance of wildflowers—from the brilliantly colored Indian paint brush and Turk's-cap lily to the showy bloodroot and pale Indian pipe. From early spring to late autumn, there is an exciting and colorful parade of wildflowers along the entire length of the Parkway, and it changes day by day and mile by mile. I promise that the joy of each new discovery will so intensify your association with nature that rather than being a mere spectator, you will come to feel a part of it yourself.

How to Use This Book

This book has been created to introduce Parkway visitors to some of the myriad and beautiful mountain wildflowers of the Parkway. By matching the flowers you see with the color photographs in this book, you will be directed to descriptions that include the names, histories, and special characteristics of each of 205 pictured species, such as how many of them were used by early human inhabitants of the Blue Ridge—for food, medicines, and magic.

Botanists, like all scientists, have developed their own professional language, which for them is necessary and valuable. For the layperson, however, such terminology can seem a nightmare. As much as possible I have written plant descriptions in common, everyday terms. However, there are times when botanical terms are needed to make the descriptions more meaningful and precise. These terms are included in a short glossary and should not distract from the purpose of this book, which is to further your enjoyment of wildflowers.

Although formal plant nomenclature can be confusing to the layperson, it has one great advantage: a plant's botanical name rarely changes over time or by region. For instance, the botanical name for Virgin's Bower is, always has been, and probably always will be *Clematis virginiana*. The common name is another story. In Vermont, it is known as Devil's Darning Needle; in some areas of the South, it is gander-vine, or it might be pipe-vine or traveler's ivy. The common names used in this book are in accordance with the *Manual of Vascular Flora of the Carolinas* as the first reference and *Gray's Manual of Botany* as the second reference. If a plant has other common names that are or have been used locally here in the mountains, those names are also included in the description of the plant.

The book has two sections: part 1 is a field guide that contains the photographs and descriptions of the wildflowers; part 2 is a tour guide to the 75 best locations for finding wildflowers along the Parkway. The indexes list both the sites and the common and scientific names of all 278 wildflowers described in the book. The final pages of the book provide a ruler (for use in measuring plant features) and space for recording your own personal list of Parkway wildflowers.

PART I. THE FIELD GUIDE

The field guide section of this book includes a majority of the common and many of the less common wildflowers that grow around the Parkway's overlooks, in recreation areas, and along many of the shorter, easy-to-walk trails. At the request of the National Park Service, however, no rare or endangered species have been included.

The photographs and descriptions in the field guide are organized by color, shape, and season of bloom. To identify a wildflower, follow these simple steps:

Step 1. Search for the flower by color.

The photographs in the field guide are arranged first by color: white, yellow, pink, blue, orange, red, green, and brown. Find the photographs that match the color of the flower you want to identify. Be aware, however, that some species may vary in color. For instance, depending on growing conditions, horse-nettle could range in color from pale blue, its normal color, to white. On close examination, however, specimens that appear to be one color (white, for instance) often show tinges of another color (such as blue or red), thus giving a clue as to their true color.)

Step 2. Search for the flower by shape.

Within each color section, flowers are arranged by shape. They fall into one of the following categories, which appear in the order shown below.

Simple-shaped flowers are those that tend to stand out separately on the stem, rather than in clusters, and which are radially symmetrical, usually having from four to six petals.

Daisy- and aster-like flowers have many radiating ray petals and may or may not have a button-like central disk.

Odd-shaped flowers usually have an unusual overall appearance and are often difficult to describe in terms of shape.

Rounded clusters are masses of usually small flowers tightly or loosely arranged in rounded or flat clusters atop the stem.

Elongated clusters are masses of usually small flowers either tightly or loosely arranged along the stem.

Vines and shrubs consist of climbers, runners, and multi-stemmed woody plants.

Within the appropriate shape section, find the photograph that matches the flower you want to identify.

Step 3. Search for the flower by time of bloom.

The flowers within each color and shape grouping (for instance, white simple-shaped flowers) are arranged according to the time they bloom, with the early spring bloomers being listed first and the late fall bloomers last.

When you have found a photograph that matches the flower you have seen, refer to the plant's description to confirm the identification. The page number of the description is given in the caption to the photograph.

The description lists additional characteristics of the plant, such as whether or not the leaves have teeth or are lobed or have hairs, or are arranged alternately or in pairs along the stem, and so on. Characteristics of the stem may also be described—for instance, whether it is round, as is typical of most plants, or square, typical of the mints.

Step 4. Check where the flower is growing.

The description also tells the general habitat in which the plant is usually found. If the habitat does not match—that is, if you find a specimen in a dry, open field, but the text describes its normal habitat as stream banks or marshy areas—the other characteristics should be reevaluated. All the flowers pictured in this book were photographed in their natural habitats.

PART 2. THE PARKWAY'S 75 BEST WILDFLOWER SITES

Part 2 of this book presents a map and tour guide to the 75 sites that I consider the best for finding wildflowers along the Parkway. The description of each site includes a list of the wildflowers you can expect to find blooming there during each of three blooming seasons: spring, summer, and fall. Seventeen "blue ribbon" sites are highlighted as "must see" destinations for serious flower lovers. All of the species listed in the 75 site inventories appear in the field guide section of the book.

Rules of the Road

In closing, please be reminded that National Park Service regulations must be observed along the entire length of the Parkway. All Parkway visitors are advised to learn and follow the Ten Commandments of Wildflower Conservation.

THE TEN COMMANDMENTS OF
WILDFLOWER CONSERVATION

1. Thou shalt not pick.
Because they wilt and die quickly when picked, leave the wild-flowers for the enjoyment of those who might follow you along the path.

2. Thou shalt not bend or break.
Because of the visual and aromatic beauty they contribute to the mountain landscape, do not harm the wildflowers in any way.

3. Thou shalt not trample.
Because the wildflowers stand proud and tall or lie sweet and delicate on the ground, do not crush them beneath your feet.

4. Thou shalt not dig.
Because the wildflowers are firmly anchored in the soil where they are meant to be, do not remove their roots from the ground or disturb them in any way.

5. Thou shalt not poach.
Because the wildflowers are here for all to enjoy, do nothing to steal that enjoyment away.[*]

6. Thou shalt not let pets run free.
Do not permit your pet to run free among the wildflowers or to relieve itself in areas where people might walk. Keep your pet on leash and under control.

7. Thou shalt not set fires.
Because fires carelessly lit and uncontrolled can be devastating to wildlife, light fires only in places authorized and provided by the National Park Service.

[*]Those interested in growing wildflowers can obtain seeds and/or plants from private wildflower nurseries. A listing of such nurseries, which propagate wild plants from seeds and cuttings, can be obtained by sending a self-addressed, stamped envelope to: North Carolina Botanical Gardens, University of North Carolina, Campus Box 3375, Totten Center, Chapel Hill, NC 27599-3375.

8. Thou shalt not alter the environment.
Because wildflowers are highly selective of the environment in which they grow, do not alter their environment in any way.

9. Thou shalt enjoy and preserve.
Because of your enjoyment of the wildflowers, take advantage of every opportunity to preserve and protect them.

10. Thou shalt educate.
Because of your love and appreciation of wildflowers, do your best to pass those feelings on to others.

These Ten Commandments of Wildflower Conservation are in keeping with National Park Service regulations that must be observed along the entire length of the Parkway. Remember that all plant life is strictly protected and that anyone who picks, digs up, or breaks any plants is subject to arrest and penalties. When searching for wildflowers, park your vehicle at an overlook or other designated parking area. Adherence to park regulations and courtesy to others will help ensure a pleasant and memorable visit to the wildflowers of the Blue Ridge Parkway.

PART ONE *Field Guide*

SIMPLE-SHAPED

Bloodroot *Sanguinaria canadensis*   Plate 1

Color: White

Bloom: March–May

Bloodroot is one of the Parkway's earliest and showiest wildflowers. The solitary, white, eight- to ten-petaled flower with a golden orange center can be found early in the spring on margins of fields and woods.

The bloodroot's stalk, which is only about 6 inches tall, grows from an enlarged underground stem called a rhizome. The leaves are rather large, circular in shape, and deeply lobed, with a waxy green color above and whitish below. A basal leaf often curls around the stalk.

This is the most familiar wildflower in the poppy family and takes its name from the reddish orange juice that will "bleed" from the broken stalk.

Indians called this plant *puccoon,* a name derived from the Indian word *pak,* meaning "blood" and referring to a variety of plants used for dyeing cloth and baskets. To this day bloodroot is known in some parts of its range as red puccoon. Bloodroot was also widely collected by early pioneers for dyeing and medicinal purposes. A drop of the juice on a lump of sugar served as a cough medicine. The juice however, had to be used sparingly when taken internally, because the root is slightly poisonous.

The pictured specimen was photographed near Mile 89 in Virginia.

Wood Anemone *Anemone quinquefolia*   Plate 2

Color: White

Bloom: March–May

The anemones are slender-stalked flowers, and because they tremble in even the slightest breeze, they are widely known as "windflowers." The delicate wood anemone features a solitary white flower above a whorl of three stalked, deeply divided leaves. The flower consists of four to nine (usually five) petal-like sepals and a creamy central disk. The leaves are divided into three or five sharply toothed segments.

Anemone is derived from Namaan, a Semitic name for Adonis, from whose blood the flower supposedly sprang; or it grew from Aphrodite's tears as she wept for the slain Adonis.

Wood anemones grow in rich woods, often in large colonies. The pictured specimen was photographed at Mabry Mill at Mile 176.2.

Plate 3

Sharp-lobed Liverleaf *Hepatica acutiloba*

Color: White–Pink

Bloom: March–May

This pretty little plant has 4- to 6-inch-long hairy stems supporting a single, white-to-pink flower with from five to twelve (usually five or six) petal-like sepals. The thickish, three-lobed leaves are borne on hairy stalks, and each lobe, being pointed, explains why the plant is called "sharp-lobed."

The genus name *Hepatica* means "pertaining to the liver" and refers to the shape of the leaves. This also explains the common name "liverleaf." The leaves are persistent through the winter, with new ones appearing after the flowers have bloomed. As you might imagine, early herbalists considered this plant to be highly useful in treating liver ailments. The Cherokee Indians took a different view of this plant. They believed that "those who dream of snakes may drink a decoction of this herb to produce vomiting, after which the dreams will not return." In the North Carolina mountains it was once thought that a girl could infallibly win the love of a sweetheart by secretly throwing over his clothing some of the powder made by rubbing together a few of the leaves dried by the fire.

Whether you want to treat your liver, win the love of a sweetheart, stop dreaming about snakes, or just enjoy its beauty, the sharp-lobed liverleaf can be found in the rich mountain woodlands. The pictured specimen was photographed at the Raven Fork View at Mile 469.8.

Wild Strawberry *Fragaria virginiana*   Plate 4

Color: White

Bloom: March–June

The wild strawberry grows close to the ground on short stems growing from long underground runners. The flower clusters and leaves appear on separate stems. Each of the three to five flowers in a cluster is about ¾ inch across and has five oval-shaped, white petals. The cone-shaped central disk is yellow, and it is from this disk that the berry develops. The leaf blades are divided into three leathery, ovate, and sharply toothed leaflets. The sweet, fleshy fruit is covered with tiny seeds and is a delicacy sought out by people as well as a variety of wild birds and animals.

A much rarer species, the wood strawberry (*F. vesca*), can be found on Grandfather Mountain. It is similar to the wild strawberry, but its flowers and fruits are smaller and are usually above the leaves. Its leaves are also more pointed.

Wild strawberries are fairly common in old fields and open areas along the Parkway. The pictured specimen was photographed at the Granite Quarry Overlook at Mile 202.8.

Giant Chickweed *Stellaria pubera*   Plate 5

Color: White

Bloom: April–May

Also known as star chickweed, this plant's ½-inch, white, starry flowers are often seen on rocky slopes early in the spring. The flower's five petals are so deeply notched that there appear to be ten. The weak stems are 4 to 10 inches long and have two vertical lines of fine hairs. The unstalked leaves are elliptic or oblong, ½ to 2 inches long, and pointed at both ends. The common chickweed

(*S. media*) is also found in scattered locations along the
Parkway. It is similar to the giant chickweed but has leafstalks supporting short, ovate leaves and floral petals that
are shorter than the sepals. The mouse-ear chickweed
(*Cerastium glomeratum*) is also similar but has hairy, sticky
stems and small, fuzzy, mouse-ear-like leaves.

Other common names for this plant include birdseed,
starweed, and winterweed. That the seeds are eaten by
several species of birds accounts for the name "birdseed."
The name "winterweed" probably comes from the plant's
ability to grow very early in the spring, even when there
is still frost on the ground. The generic name, *Stellaria*,
comes from the Latin word *stella*, meaning "star," being
descriptive of the star-like flowers.

The chickweeds are considered a delicacy in Europe,
being a good substitute for spinach. When gathered early
in the spring, before flowering, they are more tender than
any other wild green.

The pictured specimen was photographed along one of
the trails at the Cumberland Knob Visitor Center at Mile
217.5.

Plate 6 **Sweet White Violet** *Viola blanda*

Color: White

Bloom: April–May

Nearly a dozen species of violets grow in the mountains
of North Carolina and Virginia, and the sweet white violet
is one of the less common. The fragrant white flower is
about ½ inch across, and the lower petals are veined with
purple. The upper petals are pure white and often bent
backward. The leaves measure about 2½ inches across and
are shaped like a heart. The shiny, dark green color of the
leaves is an unmistakable feature of this plant.

The primrose-leaved violet (*V. primulifolia*) is also a
white violet and is scattered in various open areas along
the Parkway. It has egg-shaped leaves that narrow abruptly
toward the stalk and is usually located in moist soil.

The sweet white violet blooms in April and May and
can be found in or near the edges of rich woodlands. The

pictured specimen was photographed at the Upper Goose Creek Overlook near Mile 90 in Virginia.

Cleavers *Galium aparine*

Plate 7

Color: White

Bloom: April–May

Cleavers, also known as goosegrass, is a spreading, reclining plant characteristic of the bedstraw family to which it belongs. The weak, squarish stems are armed with stiff, backward-pointing bristles along the corners. The linear, rough, light green leaves, with bristles along the margins and the midrib, occur in whorls of six or, more typically, eight. One or two tiny, four-petaled, white flowers rise on thin stalks from the upper leaf axils. The flowers give way to small burr-like fruits that appear in pairs and are covered with short, hooked bristles, which facilitate their distribution by way of human clothing or animal fur.

This plant was widely used as a potherb in England and Scotland, where it was referred to as "clavers." This, no doubt, gave rise to its present name, "cleavers." The young spring roots are described as delicious when boiled and the seeds were roasted as a less-than-savory coffee substitute. Evidently geese also loved this bristly plant, resulting in its being called goosegrass.

Cleavers are found, usually in dense mats, at various locations along the entire length of the Parkway. The pictured specimen was photographed at the Chestnut Ridge Overlook on the Fishburn Parkway Spur Road at Mile 120.4.

May-apple *Podophyllum peltatum*

Plate 8

Color: White

Bloom: April–June

The may-apple's solitary white flower nods on a flimsy stalk beneath a pair of large, deeply lobed, umbrella-like leaves. The 2-inch-wide flower consists of from six to nine waxy, white petals. The leaves may be as large as 12 inches across.

May-apple was widely used by Indians as a remedy for a number of ailments. Early settlers considered the fruit a delicacy and also boiled the roots as a potent remedy for bronchial infections and other ailments. This might explain why the plant is also known as mandrake, a name derived from the European plant known botanically as *Mandragora officinarum*, the root of which was supposedly shaped like a human body and was a powerful and potent herb.

May-apple usually appears in large colonies in open woods or along roadsides. The pictured specimen was photographed near Rakes Mill at Mile 163.

Plate 9

Large-flowered Trillium *Trillium grandiflorum*

Color: White

Bloom: April–May

As with other trilliums, everything associated with this plant comes in threes. The large, solitary, waxy white, three-petaled flower nods on an erect stem above a whorl of three broad leaves. Peeking out from between the petals are three bright green sepals. The leaves are broadly ovate and pointed at the tip.

This is one of the stars of mountain wildflowers. In some areas the white, early-spring blossoms dot acres of the forest floor. Also known as white-lily and snow trillium, it was often used by Indians for medicinal purposes and was eaten by early settlers as cooked greens. Trillium is found growing in rich woods and on slopes. The pictured specimen was photographed near the Moses Cone Manor and Craft Shop at Mile 294.

Plate 10

Painted Trillium *Trillium undulatum*

Color: White

Bloom: April–May

This attractive trillium is easily identified by the splash of pink in the center of the white flower. An inverted pink V appears at the base of each of the three white petals. Three green sepals peek out from behind the petals. The flower is perched on an erect stalk above a whorl of three broadly ovate leaves, which are pointed at the tip.

The generic name, *Trillium*, means "three-whorl," referring to the leaves. The species name, *undulatum*, means "wavy," referring to the margins of the petals. This beautiful flower, also known as Painted Lady, grows in moist forests and thickets. The pictured specimen was photographed at the Cold Prong Pond Overlook at Mile 298.9.

Nodding Trillium *Trillium cernuum*

Plate 11

Color: White

Bloom: April–May

This is a typical trillium, with a flower consisting of three white petals in front of three green sepals and three large, diamond-shaped leaves in a whorl. This species of trillium is unique, however, in that the nodding flower is curved downward so that it hangs beneath the whorl of leaves.

Nodding trillium has a rather unpleasant odor, resulting in its being known in some areas as "Stinking Willie." It prefers a habitat of moist, acid woods and swamps. The pictured specimen was photographed in a section of low woods at Mile 333.

Bowman's-root *Gillenia trifoliata*

Plate 12

Color: White

Bloom: April–June

This erect plant has white or pinkish 1½-inch-wide flowers with five narrow, scraggly petals. The nearly stalk-less leaves are divided into three leaflets, which are 2 to 4 inches long and toothed.

The powdered root of this plant was long used by Indians and early settlers as a laxative. In fact, in some areas it is still known as Indian-physic. The origin of the name "bowman's-root" is unclear. The term "bowman" might well refer to the man at the bow of a boat. On the other hand, it might refer to an Indian, the man with a bow. In either case, the bowman had some sort of relationship with this plant's roots.

Bowman's-root grows in rich wooded areas throughout the mountains of North Carolina and Virginia. The pictured specimen was photographed along the trail to the Fox Hunter's Paradise Overlook at Mile 218.7.

Plate 13
Spotted Wintergreen *Chimaphila maculata*

Color: White

Bloom: May–June

Spotted wintergreen, also known as striped wintergreen or pipsissewa, has fragrant, waxy, white flowers nodding at the top of a 3- to 9-inch-tall stem. The evergreen leaves are conspicuous in winter as well as summer because of a contrasting white stripe along the midvein.

This plant was held in high esteem among Indian tribes because of its medicinal qualities. In fact, the name pipsissewa comes from the Cree Indian name *pipssisi kweu*, meaning "it breaks into small pieces," because it was believed to be effective in breaking down kidney stones. Also a decoction of the plant was used quite successfully to calm severe cases of hysteria. Physicians among the early European settlers agreed that this plant was a valuable tonic for certain emotional disorders.

Spotted wintergreen is common in upland conifer and hardwood forests and can be found along many of the Parkway's wooded trails. The pictured specimen was photographed along the trail near the Falling Waters Cascade Parking Area at Mile 83.3.

Plate 14
Thimbleweed *Anemone virginiana*

Color: White

Bloom: May–July

This is but one of several species of anemone called thimbleweed, because of small, dried, single-seeded fruits that are crowded on a long thimble-like receptacle. This thimbleweed, often known as tall anemone, is a rather hairy plant with three to nine greenish white or sometimes pure white flowers on a stem with several pairs, or whorls, of deeply cut leaves. Each flower is about 1 inch across and has four to nine (usually five) petal-like sepals. Petals are absent. The leaves are up to 3 inches long and are divided into segments that are wedge-shaped, toothed, and lobed.

Other names for this plant include Virginia thimble-weed, tumbleweed, and windflower. Some Indian tribes made a poultice of the leaves to treat burns, and other tribes used the woolly fruits as good luck charms.

Thimbleweeds grow in dry open areas and thickets, with the flowers appearing from late May through July. The pictured specimen was photographed at the Sheet's Gap Overlook near Mile 253.

Bladder Campion *Silene cucubalus*

Plate 15

Color: White

Bloom: May–August

Bladder campion features a loose cluster of white flow-ers, with each flower having five deeply notched petals and an inflated, bladder-like calyx that is conspicuously veined. The leaves are up to 4 inches long, oblong to lanceolate, and often clasp the stem.

As you might imagine, this plant has a number of names that refer to its conspicuous inflated bladder, including bird's-eggs, fairy-potatoes, and rattle-bags. The leaves, when boiled, have the flavor of peas and were savored by Indians and early settlers.

Bladder campion is chiefly a mountain species and can be found growing in fields and along roadsides. The pictured specimen was photographed at the Sling's Gap Overlook at Mile 132.9.

Starry Campion *Silene stellata*

Plate 16

Color: White

Bloom: July–September

The deeply fringed, five-petaled, white flowers of this plant are perched atop tall slender stalks. Each flower is about ¾ inch across, with fringed, white petals and closely grouped, bell-shaped sepals at the base. The leaves measure 1½ to 4 inches long, are smooth and lanceolate, and usually occur in whorls of four.

At one time it was believed that parts of this plant were effective antidotes to the bite of the rattlesnake and the copperhead. However, in 1842, Asa Gray of Jefferson, North Carolina, proclaimed, "This and nearly all the reputed antidotes are equally inert," meaning, of course, that they just don't work.

Starry campion inhabits rich-soiled woodlands in a variety of places along the Parkway. The pictured specimen was photographed at the Grandfather Mountain View Parking Area at Mile 307.5.

Plate 17 **White Campion** *Lychnis alba*

Color: White

Bloom: July–October

Also known as evening lychnis, this plant is an import from the Old World that is now widely distributed in North America. The much-branched stem is downy and somewhat sticky and supports a white, sweet-scented flower that is situated atop an inflated green base or calyx. Each flower is about 1 inch across and has five deeply notched petals. Male and female flowers grow on separate plants. The blossoms open at dusk and close the following morning; hence they are pollinated by night-flying moths.

A member of the pink family, a grouping of herbs that includes about 80 genera and 2,000 species, white campion grows in fields, along roadsides, and in open woods. The pictured specimen was photographed at the Peaks of Otter Picnic Area near Mile 86.

Plate 18 **Lesser Stitchwort** *Stellaria graminea*

Color: White

Bloom: May–August

Also known as common stitchwort, this import from Europe is now naturalized in this country and belongs to the chickweed family. Its small, white, star-like flowers have five petals that are so deeply notched that they appear as ten. The petals are backed by five sharply pointed sepals. The numerous flowers appear at ends of weak, spreading, diffusely branched stems, which reach a height of about 20 inches. The leaves are small, narrow, three-nerved, and stalkless.

This plant is aptly described by its generic name *Stellaria*, meaning "star-like," and its species name *graminea*, meaning "grass-like." Both names are derived from Latin terms. In Europe, parts of the plant were ground into powder, dissolved in wine, and taken to relieve the pains of "stitches," an old-world term for pains in the side.

Lesser stitchwort can be found growing in fields and along roadsides. The pictured specimen was photographed at the Little Glade Mill Pond at Mile 230.

Peruvian Daisy *Galinsoga ciliata*   Plate 19

Color: White

Bloom: May–September

This low-growing herb has small inconspicuous flowers amid an abundance of leaves. Each flower is only about ¼ inch across, with five tiny, well-spaced, three-lobed, white petals. The central floral disk is yellow. The paired, broad, toothed, and abundant leaves grow on hairy stems.

The Peruvian daisy grows in gardens, fields, barnyards, and waste areas. The pictured specimen was photographed growing under a split-rail fence at the Raven Rock Overlook near Mile 289.

White Avens *Geum canadense*   Plate 20

Color: White

Bloom: June–August

This is a slender, angular plant with small, white-petaled flowers rising from the branch tips and the leaf axils. The five petals are well spaced, with the gaps being filled by five sharply pointed, bright green sepals. The petals are as long as or longer than the sepals. The leaves, except for the simple upper ones, are divided into three or five toothed leaflets.

A similar species, the rough avens (*G. virginianum*), is also found along the Parkway. Its flowers have creamy white or pale yellow petals that are shorter than the sepals.

In early times, this plant was known by such names as cramproot and throatroot, indicating that it might have had some medicinal value to early settlers. It is reported to have a pleasant flavor and was added to ale to prevent it from going sour.

White avens grows in moist, shaded habitats. The pictured specimen was photographed in the Peaks of Otter Picnic Area at Mile 86.

Plate 21   **Jimsonweed** *Datura stramonium*

Color: White

Bloom: August–October

The handsome, white, trumpet-like flowers of the jimsonweed belie its true nature—despite its beauty, it is a foul-smelling, extremely poisonous plant. The 5-inch-long flowers, which emerge from 2-inch green sheaths, stand proudly among large, deep green, coarsely toothed leaves. As the plant matures, the flowers give way to fruit in the form of prickly, egg-shaped capsules. This plant rises on pale-green-to-purplish stems to a height of from 1 to 5 feet.

Among the earliest references to the plant is a 1676 report from Jamestown, Virginia, describing the strange behavior of soldiers who ate a boiled salad made with the leaves of "Jamestown-weed." In some parts of Virginia and North Carolina it is still known as Jamestown-weed.

All parts of this plant are toxic and cattle and sheep have been known to die from grazing on it. Cases have also been reported of children being poisoned by eating the fruit. Also, touching the leaves and flowers may cause dermatitis in susceptible persons.

Jimsonweed is found in fields, barnyards, and waste places. The pictured specimen was photographed at Sunset Fields at Mile 78.4.

Ox-eye Daisy *Chrysanthemum leucanthemum* Plate 22

Color: White

Bloom: April–July

This is the common white-and-yellow daisy of the fields and meadows bordering the Parkway. Its solitary flower is perched atop a slender, erect, 1- to 3-foot stem. The flower heads are 1 to 2 inches across and consist of numerous white rays surrounding a yellowish central disk that is slightly depressed at the center. The leaves are dark green and coarsely toothed or pinnately lobed. The lower, or basal, leaves measure to 6 inches long, while the upper leaves are only about 3 inches long.

The ox-eye daisy has many different names in this country as well as in England from whence the plant was exported to America in 1631. One of the most unusual names is maudlin daisy, commemorating Mary Magdalene, one of the witnesses to the Resurrection of Jesus Christ. According to Christian lore, Mary Magdalene credited this plant with medicinal powers, especially as a diuretic tonic. In America the plant has been successfully employed in checking the night sweats associated with pulmonary consumption.

Ox-eye daisies can be found growing in fields and pastures and along roadsides. The pictured specimen was photographed in the Peaks of Otter Park at Mile 89.

Fleabane *Erigeron spp.* Plate 23

Color: White

Bloom: April–October

There are four similar species of fleabane found in the mountains and all feature the characteristic fleabane flower heads, which consist of a yellowish central disk surrounded by as many as 100 radiating petals ranging in color from white to violet.

Common to two species are bristly, long-stalked basal leaves that are broad toward the tip (spade-like) and shallowly toothed. Common fleabane (*E. philadelphicus*) has narrow upper leaves that clasp the stem and numerous flower heads with white-to-pale-pink ray petals that are as long as the central disk is wide. Robin's-plantain (*E. pulchellus*) has narrow, nonclasping stem leaves and fewer flower heads, with pale-pink-to-violet ray petals.

Common to two other species are basal leaves that are similar to but larger than the upper stem leaves and numerous flower heads with white ray petals that are short in comparison to the width of the central disk. Daisy fleabane (*E. annuus*) has a conspicuously hairy stem, especially toward the base. *E. strigosus*, also called daisy fleabane, has stem hairs that are barely visible.

Early settlers placed dried fleabane leaves in mattresses to ward off fleas, though some old-timers say it attracted more than it repelled.

Fleabanes can be found in open woodlands, fields, and meadows and along roadsides from April to October. The pictured specimen, a common fleabane, was photographed at the Smart View Overlook at Mile 154.1.

Plate 24 **Mayweed** *Anthemis cotula*

Color: White

Bloom: May–July

This is a bushy, daisy-like plant with white ray petals surrounding a dome-shaped yellow disk. Close examination of the disk flowers will show them to be interspersed with chaff (dry, scale-like material). This is characteristic of the species, as are the numerous 1- to 1½-inch-long, finely dissected, fern-like leaves. The leaves have a rather unpleasant odor and an acrid taste.

Mayweed, which grows to a height of 1 to 2 feet, is an introduced, bushy annual that can cause skin irritation when its foliage is handled. Because it closely resembles wild chamomile, the plant from which chamomile tea is made, it is also known by another common name, "stinking chamomile."

This plant can be found in unmowed grassy areas bordering overlooks and parking areas. The pictured specimen was photographed at the Yonahlossee Overlook near Mile 304.

Wild Quinine *Parthenium integrifolium* Plate 25

Color: White

Bloom: June–August

This plant features numerous flat-topped clusters of small white flowers atop a sturdy, 2- to 3-foot-tall stem. The flowers deserve special attention because each consists of a central disk surrounded by five petals that are so small (a mere $1/16$ inch long) that they could easily be overlooked. The leaves are elliptic to lanceolate and finely toothed. The basal leaves are long-stalked and much broader than the stem leaves.

As its name suggests, wild quinine has been used for medicinal purposes in times past. Early frontier doctors found that a decoction made from the leaves was useful in treating infections of the urinary tract and the kidneys. Despite its name, however, it was never found to be a suitable substitute for quinine.

Although this plant is not considered to be a mountain species, it can be found at scattered locations along the Parkway. The pictured specimen was photographed at the Black Rock View at Mile 80.

White-flowered Aster *Aster spp.* Plate 26

Color: White

Bloom: August–Frost

Asters are usually associated with the color blue. However, nearly half of the twenty species of high-country asters are white. Typically, the blossoms consist of numerous white rays (up to 100) surrounding a yellowish central disk. Most species reach a height of 1 to 3 feet, but some grow to 7 feet. The flowers are arranged in loose clusters of from three to thirty or more. The differences in the species are usually in the shape and structure of the leaves, and positive identification is often difficult, even for botanists.

Taken from Latin and Greek, aster means "star," and the plant was so named for its star-like floral heads. Various species of asters were important sources of food and medicine for Indians and early settlers. The leaves were cooked and eaten as greens, and young roots were used to make a tea to bathe the head for headaches. The dried leaves were often burned to produce an aromatic smoke.

The species most frequently encountered along the Parkway include the white wood aster (*A. divaricatus*), the heath aster (*A. pilosus*), and the flat-topped aster (*A. umbellatus*). Asters normally grow in open woodlands and clearings and along streams. The pictured white wood aster was photographed at the Linn Cove Information Center at Mile 302.

ODD-SHAPED

Plate 27

Dutchman's-breeches *Dicentra cucullaria*

Color: White

Bloom: April–May

This plant's fragrant, white, pantaloon-shaped flowers are clustered on a leafless stalk arching over a bed of much-divided, feathery leaves. The flowers are ¾ inch long with four petals. The two outer petals have inflated spurs, which form the V that results in the unique floral shape. The grayish green leaves are long-stalked with deeply divided leaflets, resulting in the feathery appearance.

This plant is also known in some locales as stagger-weed because it is somewhat toxic to grazing animals, causing them to stagger as if intoxicated. It is found in rich woods and along stream banks. If you find it growing on a slope, it will no doubt be a north slope. The pictured specimen was photographed near the path of an old logging railroad across the Parkway from the Balsam Gap Overlook at Mile 359.9.

Indian Pipe *Monotropa uniflora* Plate 28

Color: White–Pink

Bloom: June–October

Because this strange, ghostly looking plant lacks chlorophyll, it is translucent, waxy white, and sometimes pinkish. The solitary flower with four or five petals nods at the end of a thick, scaly, 4- to 10-inch-long stalk. Leaves are not evident because they are reduced to nothing more than scales on the stalk. Plants like the Indian pipe are called saprophytes, meaning that they obtain nourishment from decaying vegetable matter in the soil through a fungal relationship associated with the roots.

Because of its color and the fact that it is cold to the touch and turns black when picked, Indian pipes are also known by such names as corpse plant, ice plant, and ghost flower. However, because the upright stalk and the drooping flower resemble a peace pipe, we have the name Indian pipe. After the drooping flower has set its seeds, it stands upright and turns a light shade of pink.

This plant is usually found in colonies in moist, rich soil under a dense canopy of trees. The pictured specimen was photographed along the trail leading to the Linn Cove Viaduct Observation Platform near the Linn Cove Information Center at Milepost 302.

ROUNDED CLUSTERS

Plantain-leaved Pussytoes *Antennaria plantaginifolia* Plate 29

Color: White

Bloom: March–June

This is a fairly low-growing plant that is often found in dense colonies. The slender, erect, and woolly stem supports a terminal cluster of fuzzy, white flower heads. Each flower head is about ½ inch wide and consists of all disk flowers enclosed by greenish or brownish bracts. The silky basal leaves are long-stalked and spoon-shaped with three to five parallel veins. The stem leaves are lance-shaped and more or less hug the stem.

It has been said that early American Indians would, for a small fee, allow themselves to be bitten by a rattlesnake and then, supposedly, would immediately cure themselves with a decoction of this herb, which they called *sinjachu*.

Plantain-leaved pussytoes grows in dry areas in woodlands, thickets, and clearings. The pictured specimen was photographed along the Parkway at Mile 123.

Plate 30

Garlic Mustard *Alliaria petiolata*

Color: White

Bloom: April–May

This 1- to 3-foot-tall plant features a small cluster of white, four-petaled flowers atop a smooth stem. The triangular leaves are up to 4 inches long, with wavy, sharply toothed margins. When crushed, the leaves give off a strong garlic odor.

This plant came to America from England, where it was known as poor man's mustard. The poor people of the countryside ate the garlic-flavored leaves as a substitute for lettuce and relish. Colonial Virginians used the leaves and seeds to make a delicious meat sauce.

Garlic mustard is found in small, scattered, isolated colonies along the northern section of the Parkway in Virginia. It normally grows in waste places and woodland edges and along roadsides. The pictured specimen was photographed at the Bull Run Knob Overlook at Mile 133.6.

Plate 31

Sweet Cicely *Osmorhiza claytonii*

Color: White

Bloom: April–May

The sparse, flat-topped clusters of this soft, hairy plant consist of tiny, white, five-petaled flowers. The alternate, widely ovate, fern-like leaves are divided three times into ovate, bluntly toothed segments.

Because the roots of this plant have a licorice- or anise-like odor and taste, it is often called anise-root. In times gone by, the roots and the spicy green fruits were often chewed by young boys. The generic name, *Osmorhiza*, is from the Greek *osmi*, meaning "scent," and *rhiza*, meaning "root." The species name, *claytonii*, honors John Clayton, who until his death in 1773 was a pioneer Virginia botanist.

Sweet cicely is chiefly a mountain species and is found in mixed deciduous forests and low woodlands. The pictured specimen was photographed at the Grandfather Mountain Parking Overlook at Mile 306.6.

Early Meadow Rue *Thalictrum dioicum*

Plate 32

Color: White

Bloom: April–May

This is a tall (2 to 8 feet), early-blooming plant with distinctive drooping flowers and foliage. The flowers appear to have three or four greenish white petals, which are in fact sepals. Many thread-like stamens hang downward from the center of each flower. The compound leaves are divided into three or five olive green, roundish, three-lobed leaflets.

This interesting plant, also known as feathered columbine and quicksilver-weed, was used by early settlers to ease the pain of sciatica and snakebites. It was also said to have made a very good quality "spruce beer." When placed in water, the leaves appear silvery, giving rise to the name quicksilver-weed.

Early meadow rue grows in rich woods and on seepage slopes. The pictured specimen was photographed at the Mahogany Rock Overlook at Mile 235.

Toothwort *Cardamine diphylla*

Plate 33

Color: White–Pink

Bloom: April–May

The toothworts are dainty spring flowers of wooded slopes and ravines. Also known as pepperwort or crinkleroot, this plant has a terminal cluster of small, four-petaled, white flowers, which turn pinkish with age. Its pair of nearly opposite leaves are each divided into three broad, toothed leaflets. A similar species, the cut-leaved toothwort (*C. concatenata*), is also found in the mountains but has a whorl of three leaves, each of which is divided into three narrow, sharply lacerated segments.

While the toothworts belong to the genus *Cardamine*, it is divided into the subgenus *Dentaria*, which includes the toothworts, and the subgenus *Cardamine*, which includes a number of species of bitter cress.

The name toothwort results from small, tooth-like swellings on the roots. The roots were relished by Indians, who cooked them with corn and described them as being very tasty as well as being good medicine for the stomach.

The pictured specimen of toothwort was photographed at the River Bend Parking Area at Linville Falls at Mile 316.5.

Plate 34   **Wild Stonecrop** *Sedum ternatum*

Color: White

Bloom: April–June

This is a low-lying plant with stems that creep along the ground sending up erect stalks. Atop the stalks are three curved or horizontal branches of floral sprays. Each flower has five sharply pointed, star-like petals, giving the sprays a feathery appearance. The leaves are small, rounded, toothless, and fleshy and usually appear in whorls of three.

Wild stonecrop was brought to this country from Europe, where it was considered an important medicinal herb because of its reported diuretic effects. Also, in England, parts of the plant were applied to the skin to remove ulcers and warts.

This species grows in damp places, usually among limestone rocks or on mossy banks along stream beds. The pictured specimen was photographed at the edge of a stream along the Trail of Trees at the James River Visitor Center at Mile 63.6.

Speckled Wood-lily *Clintonia umbellulata* Plate 35

Color: White

Bloom: May–June

The speckled wood-lily, also known as white clintonia, is one of two species of the genus *Clintonia* found along the Parkway. The other is the yellow-flowered bluebead-lily (*C. borealis*). Both species have from three to five elliptic, 4- to 12-inch-long leaves, which taper toward the base. The speckled wood-lily has a single, erect, slightly hairy stem topped by a rounded cluster of small, fragrant flowers with white petals and sepals, which are often tipped or speckled with green or purple. By midsummer the flowers give way to clusters of small dark blue or black berries.

The *Clintonia* genus was named in honor of New York Governor DeWitt Clinton (1769–1828), who was responsible for the construction of the Erie Canal and who wrote several books on natural history.

The clintonias were of limited use to Indians and early settlers. Young leaves were boiled and served as a potherb, and the berries may have been used to dye materials.

Speckled wood-lilies grow in deciduous or mixed, moist, mountain woodlands. The pictured specimen was photographed along the trail from the parking area to the Cascades at Mile 272.

Umbrella-leaf *Diphylleia cymosa* Plate 36

Color: White

Bloom: May–June

This plant's loose cluster of white flowers rises above very large, coarsely toothed leaves that are cleft into two segments. The leaves vary in size, but the leaf opposite the flower stalk is always the largest. The individual flowers are often referred to as the flowers of sixes because they consist of six petals, six sepals, and six stamens.

Umbrella-leaf is an uncommon mountain species that grows in moist, mixed woods, usually along streams or on seepage slopes. The pictured specimen was photographed along the trail to the Linn Cove Viaduct Observation Platform at Mile 304.7.

Plate 37

Cow Parsnip *Heracleum lanatum*

Color: White

Bloom: May–July

This huge, rank-smelling plant, sometimes known as masterwort, is capable of reaching a height of 10 feet or more. The stem is grooved, woolly, and hollow and is topped with large clusters of small, white, asymmetrical flowers. Each flower has five petals that are notched at the tips and often tinged with purple. The large leaves are divided into three toothed and lobed, maple-like leaflets. The stalk at the base of each leaf has an inflated sheath.

Indians often ate the spring stalks of this plant after roasting them over hot coals. Early settlers cooked and dried the roots to be used as a salt substitute, and the young roots and stems were boiled and eaten. However, because the plant resembles the deadly water hemlock, great care was taken to ensure that the plant was properly identified.

Cow parsnip grows along stream banks (as does the water hemlock), in meadows, and along roadsides. The pictured specimen was photographed at the Licklog Gap Overlook at Mile 435.9.

Plate 38

Pigeonberry *Phytolacca americana*

Color: White

Bloom: June–Frost

Pigeonberry, sometimes referred to as pokeweed or just plain poke, is an abundant, tall, large-leaved plant with reddish stems and long, arching clusters of small white flowers. Each flower is about ¼ inch across with five white petal-like sepals. Petals are absent. The leaves are up to 10 inches long, are elliptic to lanceolate, and taper at both ends. As the plant matures, the flowers give way to small green berries, which ripen to a dark purple or black.

This plant has been widely used for food and medicinal

purposes. Early settlers cooked the springtime leaves and stems and ate them as greens. It was believed that pigeonberry greens revived the blood, and since it is full of vitamin C and iron, it could be quite beneficial. The root of this plant is poisonous, and after the berries ripen the entire plant becomes poisonous and should not be eaten.

Indians made use of the berries for staining and dying. This might account for it often being called inkberry. It was an old custom among mountain folks to wear a string of pigeonberries to ward off contagious diseases. At one time the berry juice was even used to improve the taste of cheap wine.

Pigeonberry is frequently seen in open fields and waste areas. The pictured specimen was photographed at the Carrol Gap Overlook near Mile 278.

Queen Anne's Lace *Daucus carota*

Plate 39

Color: White

Bloom: June–September

Queen Anne's Lace is one of the most visible and best known of the summer wildflowers. Its tall, rough, and hairy stem supports its easily recognized lacy, flat-topped cluster of creamy white flowers. A close look at the cluster often will reveal one dark reddish brown floret in the center. This gives rise to the story that while the queen was making lace, she pricked her finger with a needle and the reddish brown floret represents a drop of the queen's blood.

This plant is a member of the parsley family and its 2- to 8-inch-long, finely cut leaves very much resemble parsley. The true nature of the plant however, can be seen in its carrot-like root. As a matter of fact, it is a wild carrot and is often known by that name. Because the root is rich in carotin, it does have some healing powers. Old woodsmen often grated the root and mixed it with oil for a soothing application to burns. The plant also has a reputation for curing internal disorders, and although the blossoms are not usually eaten, the central reddish brown floret was once thought to cure epilepsy. The grated root and juice can be and often is eaten.

Queen Anne's Lace is abundant in open fields and along roadsides. The pictured specimen was photographed at the Northwest Trading Post at Mile 259.

Plate 40

Poke Milkweed *Asclepias exaltata*

Color: White

Bloom: June–July

Poke milkweed is an erect, 3- to 6-foot-tall plant with opposite, lanceolate leaves that sometimes reach a length of 8 inches and are tapered to a point at both ends. Typical of the milkweeds, this plant "bleeds" a milky white juice when injured or broken. The flowers, which appear in drooping clusters, have five distinctive, sharply reflexed petals supporting a crown of five tiny, hooded, and incurved horns.

During World War II, cottony floss from milkweed seedpods was in high demand for making life preservers and aviator's flying suits. The floss is considered as warm as wool yet six times lighter and is five to six times as buoyant as cork.

Poke milkweed is chiefly a mountain species found in hardwood forests and along forest edges. The pictured specimen was photographed along the Figure 8 Trail at the Moses Cone Manor and Craft Shop at Mile 294.

Plate 41

Catnip *Nepeta cataria*

Color: White

Bloom: June–August

There are numerous members of the mint family growing along the Parkway, and catnip is one of them. This hairy plant with a tantalizing odor has spotted, pale white flowers clustered atop the main stem and branches. Each of the tubular flowers is two-lipped, the smaller, upper lip being notched at the tip and the larger, lower lip having two lateral lobes. Four stamens are arched beneath the upper lip. The arrowhead-shaped leaves are opposite and coarsely toothed and, like the squarish stem, are covered with a grayish down.

Catnip has no known therapeutic virtues for humans, but its odor drives cats wild. It contains a terpene-like chemical, nepeta lactone, which seems to repel insects, and has an interesting effect on the behavior of cats. Catnip is common in the mountains, growing along roadsides and in pastures. The pictured specimen was photographed at the Afton View at Mile 0.2.

Yarrow *Achillea millefolium*

Plate 42

Color: White

Bloom: June–September

This aromatic plant, often referred to as milfoil, has feathery, fern-like leaves. Its fibrous stem is topped with a flattish cluster of small white flowers. Each flower is ¼ to ½ inch across and has three to five roundish ray petals surrounding a cream-colored central disk.

Because of the feathery appearance of this plant, it is known in some areas as *plumajillo*, or "little feather." In other areas it is known as nosebleed, because of its irritating odor. Early settlers steeped the leaves in boiling water and used the resulting brew to treat cuts and bruises and to stop bleeding.

Yarrow blooms throughout the summer months and can readily be seen alongside the Parkway, in picnic areas, and in open fields. The pictured specimen was photographed at the Stone Mountain Overlook at Mile 232.5.

Water Hemlock *Cicuta maculata*

Plate 43

Color: White

Bloom: June–September

This 3- to 6-foot-tall member of the parsley family has a smooth, stout stem streaked with purple. The leaves are double or triple compound, coarsely toothed, and often have a reddish tinge. The small white flowers appear in dome-shaped clusters at the ends of the upper branches. The umbels formed by the clusters are similar to but smaller and looser than those of the Queen Anne's Lace.

The poison from this plant is extremely powerful and a small amount can be fatal. In early times the roots were sometimes mistaken for parsnips and other root crops, with fatal results. When the Greek philosopher Socrates was condemned to death by Athenian officials for his unpopular teachings, he killed himself by drinking a poisonous potion said to have been laced with juices from the water hemlock.

This plant grows in wet meadows and along streams. The pictured specimen was photographed on the edge of a stream in the picnic area at the Peaks of Otter Recreation Area near Mile 86.

Plate 44 **Flowering Spurge** *Euphorbia corollata*

Color: White

Bloom: June–October

This smooth plant with leafy stems will grow to a height of up to 3 feet. A flat "umbrella" of flowers rises on five or six stalks above a whorl of small leaves. What appear to be five-petaled white flowers are really not flowers at all; they are cup-shaped structures that contain the flowers. The white, so-called "petals" are actually lobes on the rim of the cup, and each lobe has a yellowish green gland at the base. The leaves, except for the ones in the whorl, are alternate, elliptic, and 1 to 2 inches long. Like other true spurges, this plant contains a milky juice.

During the early 1800s it was reported that this plant was used by Indians to purge the body of poisons through vomiting. In 1817, a Dr. Bigelow reported that flowering spurge must undoubtedly be ranked among the most efficient medicines for evacuating the digestive system. It is not surprising that the Indian name for this plant, *peheca*, translated to "go quick."

Flowering spurge, which is sometimes known as tramp's spurge, grows in open woods and fields and along roadsides. The pictured specimen was photographed at the Sheet's Gap Overlook at Mile 252.8.

Hoary Mountain Mint *Pycnanthemum incanum* Plate 45

Color: White

Bloom: July–September

Hoary mountain mint is a perennial herb with a spearmint-like odor so pungent that the plant can easily be identified by smell alone. It grows to a height of 2 feet and often appears in large creamy white colonies as pleasing to the eye as to the nose.

The plant's small white-to-lavender flowers form dense rounded clusters that grow from the upper leaf axils or at the top of the hairy, square stem. Each flower has two lips, the lower of which is spotted with purple. The leaves are opposite, up to 2 inches long, and have widely spaced marginal teeth. The upper pair of leaves, just below the flower cluster, shows the same creamy white, hoarfrost color as the flower.

Hoary mountain mint grows in open woods, thickets, and fields. The pictured specimen was photographed a short distance south of the Parkway's intersection with Route 18, at Mile 248, near Laurel Springs, North Carolina.

Bouncing Bet *Saponaria officinalis* Plate 46

Color: White–Pink

Bloom: July–September

The smooth, branching stems of this member of the pink family support terminal clusters of white or sometimes pinkish flowers. Each of the fragrant flowers is about 1 inch across, with five delicately scalloped petals with small appendages at their throats. A five-lobed calyx forms a tube beneath the flower. The leaves are 2 to 3 inches long, opposite, and oval, with three to five conspicuous veins.

The Bouncing Bet is a phlox-like perennial introduced from Europe. It spreads by underground stems and often forms sizable colonies. The plant contains a poisonous, soap-like substance called saponin. This inspired the generic name *Saponaria*, from the Latin term meaning "soap." This also accounts for an alternate common name, soapwort. Though lather can be made from its crushed foliage, it is doubtful that it was ever used for washing. The name Bouncing Bet, however, comes from an old fashioned term for washerwoman.

Bouncing Bet grows along roadsides and in other disturbed areas. The pictured specimen was photographed along the abandoned Cable Car Road at Mile 234.

Plate 47
Virginia Bugleweed *Lycopus virginicus*

Color: White

Bloom: July–Frost

Though the bugleweeds are very similar in appearance to wild mint, the leaves lack the strong minty odor associated with the mints. This species, the Virginian bugleweed, grows to a height of about 2 feet and features rounded clusters of tiny, white, bugle-shaped flowers in the axils of paired leaves. The light green leaves are coarsely toothed and gradually taper at both ends. The stem is quite smooth and, like the mints, squarish.

The generic name *Lycopus* is from the Greek words *lycos*, meaning "wolf," and *pous*, meaning "foot," and refers to the likeness of the leaves of some of the *Lycopus* species to the footprint of a wolf. It is reported, but not substantiated, that a tea made from the leaves was used by early settlers as a sedative.

Virginia bugleweed grows in damp alluvial woods and wet meadows. The pictured specimen was photographed at the Little Glade Mill Pond Picnic Area at Mile 230.1.

Plate 48
Pale Indian-plantain *Cacalia atriplicifolia*

Color: White

Bloom: June–October

This striking plant has a smooth, round, and somewhat whitened stem that grows to a height of 3 to 6 feet. The numerous tubular, white flower heads are arranged in large, loose, and more or less flat-topped clusters. A row of erect bracts holds the tubular flowers closely packed in the flower heads. The leaves are large and triangular or fan-shaped, with a broad base and angular lobes. The color of the leaves is pale green above and somewhat whitish beneath.

Pale Indian-plantain grows in dry open woods and thickets and along roadsides. The pictured specimen was photographed near the rock wall across the Parkway from the Mahogany Rock Overlook at Mile 235.

Filmy Angelica *Angelica triquinata* Plate 49

Color: White

Bloom: August–September

Angelicas, of which there are several species, are so named because they supposedly begin to bloom on the feast day of St. Michael the Archangel. They are, in fact, known in England by the name Archangel. The filmy angelica's purplish, 3- to 5-foot stem is topped with flat clusters of greenish white flowers. The stalks of the upper leaves emerge from a swollen sheath, and the leaves are divided into three leaflets, which may be further divided into threes or fives. Each leaflet is thin, ovate, and coarsely toothed. The thinness of the leaves is no doubt responsible for the "filmy" part of the name.

In keeping with its "angelic" name, this has long been an interesting and useful plant. It is reported that Indians, when hunting, used this plant to lure game. The hunter would rub the root between his hands, and the resulting odor attracted deer to within range of the bow and arrows. This ploy was so effective that the Indians referred to the plant as "the hunting plant." Early settlers also found uses for angelica. Juices from the plant were used to "sweeten the breath," and the roots were rubbed on the lower parts of the legs to prevent snakebite. Even today, some old-timers carry pieces of the root for good luck.

Filmy angelica grows on rocky slopes, along stream margins, and in damp meadows. The pictured specimen was photographed at the John Rock View at Mile 419.3.

Plate 50

Boneset *Eupatorium perfoliatum*

Color: White

Bloom: August–October

This fairly tall (2 to 4 feet) member of the thoroughwort family is a hairy plant with dense, flat-topped clusters of many, small, creamy white flower heads. The 4- to 8-inch-long leaves are opposite, lanceolate, toothed, and united at the base to completely surround the stem. In fact, the species name, *perfoliatum*, translates to "through the leaf." Upland boneset (*E. sessilifolium*) is very similar except that the opposite leaves are not fused at the base. The hyssop-leaved boneset (*E. hyssopifolium*) has similar flower heads, but the numerous, linear, grass-like leaves are paired or occur in whorls of four. Often, smaller leaves rise from the axils of the larger leaves.

The Indians were the first to discover the medicinal values of this plant and named it ague-weed. They found that a tonic made from the dried leaves was effective in treating colds, coughs, and constipation. Later, early herb-doctors wrapped the leaves in bandages covering broken bones, and the plant became known as boneset. Dr. Charles F. Millspaugh, an early practitioner, noted in 1900, "there are probably no plants in American domestic medical practice that are used as extensively and frequently as the Bonesets."

Boneset inhabits alluvial woods and wet meadows. The pictured specimen was photographed at the Little Glade Mill Pond at Mile 230.1.

Plate 51

White Snakeroot *Eupatorium rugosum*

Color: White

Bloom: August–October

White snakeroot has a rough, hairy, 1- to 3-foot-tall stem that branches toward the top. Each branch supports several flower heads, each of them consisting of five to seven small, white, tubular flowers. The branched flower heads are arranged in large, rather loose, flat-topped clusters. The leaves are broadly oblong, toothed on the margins, very veiny in appearance, and from 1 to 4 inches long. The snake-like root system branches out to form large colonies.

White snakeroot contains a toxic alcohol called tremetol that causes a disease known as "milk sickness." The sickness is transmitted through the milk of cows foraging on the plant. Milk sickness decimated the farm population of the South and Midwest before white snakeroot was confirmed as the cause in 1917. Modern dairy farmers are careful to keep this plant out of their pastures, and the sickness is no longer a problem.

This plant grows in rich, mixed woods, thickets, and clearings. The pictured specimen was photographed at the Mahogany Rock Overlook at Mile 235.

Rattlesnake-root *Prenanthes spp.* Plate 52

Color: White–Pink

Bloom: August–Frost

There are several species of rattlesnake-root found along the Parkway, and they are all tall, slender plants with bell-like flowers hanging in drooping clusters and leaves of extremely variable shapes. The species pictured, called lion's-foot (*P. serpentaria*), has creamy-white-to-pinkish flowers with white, bristly, enfolding floral bracts with a creamy white pappus beneath. The upper leaves are lanceolate and slightly lobed, while the lower leaves are deeply and irregularly lobed. A similar species, gall-of-the-earth (*P. trifoliolata*), has pale-green-to-pinkish floral bracts and lower leaves divided into three distinct segments. Tall white lettuce (*P. altissima*) has only five enfolding floral bracts (other species have eight) and large triangular lower leaves.

Mountain folklore would have us believe that smearing the milky juice of the rattlesnake-root on your hands will prevent the bite of poisonous snakes. In the unfortunate event that you should be bitten, however, drink the milky juice and apply rattlesnake-root leaves to the wound. This was said to be an excellent antidote.

Rattlesnake-roots are usually found in shaded areas

of open woods or along stream banks. The lion's-foot pictured was photographed at the Little Glade Mill Pond Picnic Area at Mile 230.1.

ELONGATED CLUSTERS

Plate 53 **Bitter Cress** *Cardamine spp.*

Color: White

Bloom: March–May

A number of early-blooming species of bitter cress appear along the length of the Parkway. All belong to the mustard family, and most have small terminal clusters of tiny white or pink four-petaled flowers and slender ascending seedpods.

Hairy bitter cress (*C. hirsuta*) is freely branched at the base and rises from a rosette of 2- to 3-inch-long leaves, which are deeply lobed into one to four pairs of elliptic divisions. The slender seedpods extend upward beyond the floral cluster. This species is found in disturbed areas, especially around overlooks and parking areas.

Pennsylvania bitter cress (*C. pensylvanica*) is usually found in wet, mostly wooded habitats, often in water. It is similar to *C. hirsuta* but has a thicker stem with stiff, bristly hairs. The small-flowered bitter cress (*C. parviflora*), with its slender stem and 1½-inch-long stem leaves divided into narrow segments, is a plant of the fields, sandy woods, and occasionally wet cliffs and flat granite outcrops.

The pictured specimen of hairy bitter cress was photographed at the Smart View Overlook at Mile 154.2.

Plate 54 **Shepherd's-purse** *Capsella bursa-pastoris*

Color: White

Bloom: March–June

Also known as shepherd's-pouch, this common weed grows to a height of 6 to 20 inches. The small white flowers are arranged on a long, slender spike and bloom upward, leaving heart-shaped seedpods as they go. The base leaves are similar to those of a dandelion and the upper leaves are lance-shaped, clasping the stem.

The generic name *Capsella* means "little box," referring to the heart-shaped seedpods, and the species name *bursa-pastoris*, again referring to the seedpods, means "purse of the shepherd."

Shepherd's-purse is a member of the mustard family and grows pretty much throughout the world. In the spring it can be found growing along the Parkway in almost any field or open space or along the roadside. The pictured specimen was photographed at the Upper Goose Creek Overlook at Mile 90.

Smooth Rock-cress *Arabis laevigata*

Plate 55

Color: White

Bloom: April–May

This stiffly erect plant has elongated clusters of small bell-like flowers that at first glance appear light green. Green, however, is the color of the sepals overlapping the creamy white petals. Each of the flowers has a slender seedpod protruding from the center, and the more mature the flower, the longer the seedpod. At full maturity, the flower petals drop and the long, slender seedpod, so typical of the cresses, remains. The clasping, spatula-like leaves are toothed toward the tip and have a smooth texture, which contributes to the plant's name.

Smooth rock-cress grows in rich woods and slopes or on shaded rocky ledges. The pictured specimen was photographed at the Round Meadow Overlook at Mile 179.3.

False Solomon's-seal *Smilacina racemosa*

Plate 56

Color: White

Bloom: April–June

The long, arching stem of this plant, similar to true Solomon's seal, bears a pyramidal cluster of many small white flowers at its tip. Each of the tiny white flowers is about ⅛ inch across and consists of three petals and three petal-like sepals. The leaves are alternate, from 3 to 6 inches long, and have fine hairs on the underside and along the margins. Also the leaves have conspicuous parallel veins. The fruit consists of small berries, at first green and speckled with red and finally translucent ruby-red.

The generic name, *Smilacina*, comes from the Greek word meaning "rough" or "scraping" and refers to the hairy stem. The species name, *racemosa*, comes from the Latin and is appropriate since the flowers occur in terminal clusters or racemes. This Solomon's seal, imported from England where it is known as Job's tears, is called "false" because it apparently lacks the magical or medicinal qualities that at one time were attributed to the true Solomon's seal.

This plant is normally found in rich deciduous woods and thrives along woodland trails. The pictured specimen was photographed along the trail from the parking area to the Jumpinoff Rock Overlook near Mile 261.

Plate 57

Corn Gromwell *Lithospermum arvense*

Color: White

Bloom: April–June

Corn gromwell, also known as the "painting plant," is a rough, hairy member of the forget-me-not family. Its small, insignificant, white, five-petaled flowers are tucked among leafy bracts in the crowded, upper leaf axils. The roughened leaves are narrowly lance-shaped and sharp pointed, with only the middle vein being obvious.

On festive days, girls of Northern Europe painted their faces with juice from the roots of this plant. The root bark will tinge wax and oil a beautiful red. It was also used to color syrups, jellies, and confections. This explains the name "painting plant." The name "corn gromwell," however, is not so clear. In botany, the term "glomerule" refers to a compact cluster. So perhaps, that word evolved into "gromwell" to describe the compact cluster of leafy bracts in which the flowers appear.

This plant will be found growing in sandy fields and waste places along the Parkway. The pictured specimen

was photographed at the Stewart Knob Overlook at Mile
110.9.

White Sweet Clover *Melilotus alba*

Plate 58

Color: White

Bloom: May–September

There are two species of sweet clover that grow along
the Parkway, and except for flower color they are almost
identical. This is the white species; the other is yellow
sweet clover (*M. officinalis*).

The sweet clovers are smooth, bushy plants that grow
to a height of 3 to 6 feet. Numerous, small, clover-like
flowers are arranged in long, narrow clusters arising from
the leaf axils. The leaves are divided into three narrowly
oblong leaflets that are toothed along the margins and
around the rounded tip.

The name "sweet clover" comes from the sweet-
scented, vanilla-like odor given off by the plants when
crushed or dried. Both species of sweet clover are European natives that have become widely naturalized in
North America.

Sweet clover can be found along roadsides, in fields,
and in waste areas. The pictured specimen of white sweet
clover was photographed at the Mount Mitchell View
Parking Area near Mile 350.

Early Saxifrage *Saxifraga virginiensis*

Plate 59

Color: White

Bloom: March–May

This is one of the four species of saxifrage that could
be encountered along the Parkway. The sticky-hairy, 4- to
10-inch stem of this species rises from a rosette of broadly
toothed, ovate leaves. The five-petaled white flowers, with
ten bright yellow stamens in the center, form a cluster
atop the stem.

The name "saxifrage" is derived from the Latin terms
saxum (rock) and *frangere* (to break), as some species grow
in rock crevices and were reputed to break rocks. This also

led to the belief that a decoction brewed from the leaves would serve as a remedy for bladder and kidney stones.

Early saxifrage emerges in dry woods and rocky areas. The pictured specimen was photographed along the trail to the river shipping locks near the James River Visitor Center at Mile 63.6.

Plate 60 **Lettuce Saxifrage** *Saxifraga micranthidifolia*

Color: White

Bloom: May–June

This many-branched, 12-inch-tall plant has elongated, open clusters of small white flowers. Each flower has four to eight petals. The best identifying characteristic for this plant is its set of numerous, oblong leaves, which have as many as forty sharp teeth along each margin. The leaves gradually taper at the base into short, winged leafstalks. The more elusive Michaux saxifrage (*S. michauxii*) is similar in habitat and appearance, but its white flowers are spotted with yellow.

The genus name *Saxifraga* is derived from *saxum* (a rock) and *frangere* (to break), since some species grow in rock crevices and were believed to break rocks. This notion led to the belief that the plant was a good remedy for kidney stones. Lettuce saxifrage is a plant of the Appalachian Mountains, and over much of its range it is known as mountain lettuce. It was and still is highly prized and is probably used for salads more than any other wild plant.

Look for this plant on seepage slopes and in moist rocky places. The pictured specimen was photographed along a rocky stream near the Peaks of Otter Lodge at Mile 86.

Plate 61 **Lily of the Valley** *Convallaria montana*

Color: White

Bloom: May–June

This pretty little plant is recognized by nearly everyone. Its dainty, fragrant, white, bell-shaped flowers dangle in a long cluster beneath a canopy of one or two smooth, elliptic leaves. The leaves, which reach a length of 6 inches or more, sheathe the base of the stalk and then rise vertically and arch downward toward the tip.

This imported plant is an escapee "garden flower" that can be found in isolated pockets along the Parkway. According to European folklore, these lilies, sometimes called Lady's tears, sprang from Mary's teardrops as she wept at the foot of the cross.

The pictured specimen was photographed near the forest's edge at the Great Valley View at Mile 99.6.

False Lily of the Valley *Maianthemum canadense*

Plate 62

Color: White

Bloom: May–July

This plant's elongated cluster of four-pointed white flowers (the four points of two sepals and two petals) top a 3- to 6-inch stem that is clasped by two or three deeply cleft, heart-shaped leaves. As the plant matures, the blossoms give way to tiny red berries.

Very little is known about how this plant might have been used by the Indians and early settlers. However, one of the names often used for this plant was scurvy-berries, suggesting that the berries might have been chewed to help prevent scurvy.

This pretty little mountain wildflower grows in upland woods and thickets. The pictured specimen was photographed along the trail to the Linn Cove Viaduct Observation Platform at Mile 304.7.

Galax *Galax aphylla*

Plate 63

Color: White

Bloom: May–July

Galax is most noticed by its long-stalked, roundish, heart-shaped, and shiny leaves. They measure 1 to 3 inches across and have small bristly teeth along the edges. During the summer months, patches of galax carpet the forest floor with these bright green leaves. During the winter months the leaves become reddish or bronze. The tiny white flowers, which start to appear in May, are arranged in narrow, spike-like clusters on a naked, 10- to 18-inch, wand-like stalk. This results in the plant often being called the wandflower.

This attractive southern wildflower is found only in the Southern Appalachians. The generic name *Galax* is derived from the Greek word *gala*, meaning "milk," and refers to the milky white color of the flower.

This is a native plant of the rich, moist woods of the Blue Ridge Mountains. The pictured specimen was photographed along the trail to the Linn Cove Viaduct Observation Platform near the Linn Cove Information Center at Mile 304.7.

Plate 64 **Colicroot** *Aletris farinosa*

Color: White

Bloom: May–July

The small, urn-shaped flowers of this plant appear in spike-like clusters near the top of a sturdy stem. Each flower is only about ¼ inch long and consists of three petals and three sepals fused to form a six-lobed tube with a swollen base. The pale green, lanceolate, and long-pointed leaves are arranged in a basal rosette.

In the mid-1800s, this plant was widely used as a remedy for colic (acute abdominal pains). A decoction of the roots and leaves was administered in liberal doses despite its being described as intensely bitter. Jacob Bigelow, in his 1820 *American Medical Botany*, wrote of its intense and permanent bitterness.

Colicroot grows in meadows, old fields, and open woods. The pictured specimen was photographed at the Little Glade Mill Pond at Mile 230.

Plate 65 **Fly-Poison** *Amianthium muscaetoxicum*

Color: White

Bloom: May–August

The small white flowers of this plant grow in cylindrical clusters at the top of a mostly leafless stem. Each flower measures about ½ inch across, has three petals and three petal-like sepals, and turns a greenish purple with age. The leaves are grass-like, with the lower leaves measuring up to 12 inches long and the upper leaves being much shorter.

This plant contains a very poisonous alkaloid and has been known to cause the death of foraging livestock. At one time, a pulp from this plant was mixed with sugar and used to kill flies—hence the species name, from the Latin *muscae* (flies) and *toxicum* (poison).

Fly-poison is often found growing in meadows and on wooded slopes. The pictured specimen was photographed growing in a rocky crevasse at the summit of the Flat Rock Trial at Mile 308.2.

Smaller Enchanter's Nightshade *Circaea alpina*

Plate 66

Color: White

Bloom: June–September

This plant's tiny and delicate flowers consist of two deeply notched, white petals separated by two reflexed sepals resting atop a slightly swollen base. The flowers are arranged in a loose, elongated cluster along a slender stem. The paired leaves are somewhat heart-shaped and coarsely toothed.

Though appearing small and dainty, this plant survives in cold woods from northern Canada to the higher elevations of the North Carolina mountains. Look for it in damp, low-lying, wooded areas. The pictured specimen was photographed beneath a fence rail at the Split Rock Overlook on Grandfather Mountain at Mile 305.

Black Cohosh *Cimicifuga racemosa*

Plate 67

Color: White

Bloom: June–September

This tall, conspicuous member of the bugbane family can be found in a variety of places along the Parkway. Its 3- to 6-foot height and long, narrow, gently arching spikes of tuft-like flowers are unmistakable. Close inspection of the small white flowers shows that each consists of a tassel-like group of stamens with a pistil in the center. Some of the outermost stamens resemble petals, but there are no true petals. The leaves are large and compound, with three to five egg-shaped, sharply toothed leaflets that are pointed at the end.

In much of Appalachia, at one time, a tea was made from the root of this plant to ease symptoms of sore throat, lung infections, and various other disorders. Indians boiled the root to produce an extract to cure rheumatism and kidney infections.

Like other members of the bugbane family, this plant's unpleasant odor is said to repel insects. However, this photographer found little relief from the insects while photographing this plant.

Black cohosh grows in rich woods. The pictured specimen was photographed near the entrance to the campground at the Peaks of Otter Park near Mile 86.

Plate 68

English Plantain *Plantago lanceolata*

Color: White

Bloom: June–Frost

In many areas, this plant is considered nothing more than an obnoxious weed; on the other hand, its seeds are relished by many songbirds, and the leaves are a favorite food of wild rabbits. The basal rosette of long, narrow, strongly ribbed leaves give rise to a slender stalk, which is topped by a dense, dark green, cone-shaped head from which emerge tiny, spirally arranged, greenish white flowers. Each flower consists of a four-lobed corolla with four protruding, white stamens.

English plantain is also known as Chimney Sweep, because the flower head resembles the brushes that were once used to clean chimneys in England. This plant is widespread and grows in waste areas, in pastures, and along roadsides. The pictured specimen was photographed at the Basin Cove View at Mile 244.7.

Indian-tobacco *Lobelia inflata* Plate 69

Color: White

Bloom: July–September

Indian-tobacco is easily recognized by its small white or sometimes pale blue flowers with oval bases that become swollen like bladders as the fruit forms. The somewhat hairy and many-branched stem grows to a height of 1 to 3 feet. The light green leaves are alternate, ovate, and toothed.

The leaves of this plant have the taste of mild tobacco, and it was at one time called wild tobacco. It was presumed that any plant tasting like tobacco would naturally be used by Indians, so the wild tobacco came to be called Indian-tobacco. There is no record, however, of this plant ever being used by Indians as a tobacco. Actually, the roots of this plant are poisonous and could prove fatal if consumed in quantity.

This poisonous annual is found in a variety of habitats but most often where the soil is poor. The pictured specimen was photographed at the Chestoa View Parking Area at Mile 320.8.

Nodding Ladies' Tresses *Spiranthes cernua* Plate 70

Color: White

Bloom: August–Frost

This delicate plant, also known as pearl-twist, features small, creamy white, fragrant flowers arranged on a floral spike in spiral-like rows. The flowers are about ½ inch long with side petals and an upper sepal that unite to form ʾood over the wavy-edged lower lip. The lower leaves ʾ and grass-like, while the upper stem leaves are scales.

ʾies' tresses, also known as autumn-tresses ʾvs in fields and damp meadows. The photographed at the Wilson Creek

Plate 71

Silverrod *Solidago bicolor*

Color: White

Bloom: September–October

Because this is the only species of goldenrod with white blossoms, it is aptly called silverrod, or at times, white goldenrod.

The short-stalked, white flower heads grow in an elongated spike along the length of a grayish, hairy stem. Each of the tiny flowers has seven to nine white rays surrounding a small, yellow central disk. The 2- to 4-inch-long leaves are oblong in shape. The lower leaves are stalked and toothed while the upper leaves are smaller, narrower, and often without stalks or teeth.

This plant is found in any number of places along the Parkway, usually inhabiting open woods or dry, open pastures and meadows. The pictured specimen was photographed at the Mahogany Rock Overlook at Mile 235.

VINES AND SHRUBS

Plate 72

Flowering Dogwood *Cornus florida*

Color: White

Bloom: March–April

The flowering dogwood is a small tree, but it is included here among the wildflowers because its bright, early-season blossoms are among the first to brighten the drab winter landscape. The actual blossoms are small, greenish yellow, and centrally located amid the showy, white brac that are often mistaken for petals. The dark green, o site, and ovate leaves have veins curving toward pointed tip. The dogwood's rich red autum exceeds the beauty of its springtime blo

Flowering dogwood, the state flo can be found growing almost ar at elevations under 3,000 fe photographed at the Q

Indian-tobacco *Lobelia inflata*

Plate 69

Color: White

Bloom: July–September

Indian-tobacco is easily recognized by its small white or sometimes pale blue flowers with oval bases that become swollen like bladders as the fruit forms. The somewhat hairy and many-branched stem grows to a height of 1 to 3 feet. The light green leaves are alternate, ovate, and toothed.

The leaves of this plant have the taste of mild tobacco, and it was at one time called wild tobacco. It was presumed that any plant tasting like tobacco would naturally be used by Indians, so the wild tobacco came to be called Indian-tobacco. There is no record, however, of this plant ever being used by Indians as a tobacco. Actually, the roots of this plant are poisonous and could prove fatal if consumed in quantity.

This poisonous annual is found in a variety of habitats but most often where the soil is poor. The pictured specimen was photographed at the Chestoa View Parking Area at Mile 320.8.

Nodding Ladies' Tresses *Spiranthes cernua*

Plate 70

Color: White

Bloom: August–Frost

This delicate plant, also known as pearl-twist, features small, creamy white, fragrant flowers arranged on a floral spike in spiral-like rows. The flowers are about ½ inch long with side petals and an upper sepal that unite to form a hood over the wavy-edged lower lip. The lower leaves are long and grass-like, while the upper stem leaves are reduced to scales.

Nodding ladies' tresses, also known as autumn-tresses and hen's-toes, grows in fields and damp meadows. The pictured specimen was photographed at the Wilson Creek Overlook at Mile 303.7.

Plate 71

Silverrod *Solidago bicolor*

Color: White

Bloom: September–October

Because this is the only species of goldenrod with white blossoms, it is aptly called silverrod, or at times, white goldenrod.

The short-stalked, white flower heads grow in an elongated spike along the length of a grayish, hairy stem. Each of the tiny flowers has seven to nine white rays surrounding a small, yellow central disk. The 2- to 4-inch-long leaves are oblong in shape. The lower leaves are stalked and toothed while the upper leaves are smaller, narrower, and often without stalks or teeth.

This plant is found in any number of places along the Parkway, usually inhabiting open woods or dry, open pastures and meadows. The pictured specimen was photographed at the Mahogany Rock Overlook at Mile 235.

VINES AND SHRUBS

Plate 72

Flowering Dogwood *Cornus florida*

Color: White

Bloom: March–April

The flowering dogwood is a small tree, but it is included here among the wildflowers because its bright, early-season blossoms are among the first to brighten the drab winter landscape. The actual blossoms are small, greenish yellow, and centrally located amid the showy, white bracts that are often mistaken for petals. The dark green, opposite, and ovate leaves have veins curving toward the pointed tip. The dogwood's rich red autumn foliage almost exceeds the beauty of its springtime blossoms.

Flowering dogwood, the state flower of North Carolina, can be found growing almost anywhere along the Parkway at elevations under 3,000 feet. The pictured specimen was photographed at the Quarry Overlook at Mile 100.9.

Mountain Laurel *Kalmia latifolia*

Plate 73

Color: White

Bloom: April–June

The mountain laurel is without a doubt one of the showiest of mountain flowers. Its large clusters of white-to-rose-colored flowers, splashed with purple and accentuated by bright evergreen leaves and pink buds, help turn the springtime mountain landscape into a spectacular chorus of color.

A medium-sized shrub of the ivy family, the mountain laurel is many-branched from the base, thus forming a rounded top that can reach a height of 30 feet or more. It begins to bloom as early as April and reaches peak bloom in mid- to late May.

Because of its tolerance of shade, mountain laurel grows well in open woods, thereby providing an evergreen touch to the winter scene. This plant can be found in large clumps in a variety of places along the Parkway. The pictured specimen was photographed near the Bull Head Mountain Overlook at Mile 233.7.

Blackberry *Rubus spp.*

Plate 74

Color: White

Bloom: April–June

Blackberries, raspberries, and dewberries all belong to a large group of plants commonly known as brambles and classified under the genus name *Rubus*. All these plants have delectable fruits and come from closely related species of the rose family. Their leaves are usually compound and their thorny branches, called canes, often arch toward the ground. Brambles are divided yet further, and the blackberries fall into a subgenus called *Eubatus*.

Two principal species of blackberries are normally found along the Parkway. Both have arching, thorny canes; compound leaves divided into three or five ovate, toothed leaflets; and white, five-petaled flowers that give way to black, juicy fruits. The common blackberry (*R. argutus*) is normally found at lower altitudes, blooms in April and

May, and has thorns that are slightly curved. The high-bush blackberry (*R. allegheniensis*) is normally found at higher altitudes, blooms in May and June, and has straight thorns.

Many birds and animals, as well as people, enjoy the succulent berries, and the thick bramble patches furnish shelter for wildlife and protection for seedlings of trees and other shrubs. Blackberries grow in thickets and on woodland borders along the length of the Parkway. The pictured specimen was photographed at the Doughton Park Overlook at Mile 240.9.

Plate 75 **Squaw-huckleberry** *Vaccinium stamineum*

Color: White

Bloom: May–June

The squaw-huckleberry, also known as deerberry, is a medium-sized shrub with alternate, elliptic, untoothed leaves that taper to a point at both ends and are whitish and hairy beneath. The small, greenish white, bell-like flowers dangle in elongated clusters from the axils of leaf-like bracts. Each flower is five lobed, with yellowish stamens protruding from the center.

The genus name, *Vaccinium*, is presumably from the Latin *vaccinus*, meaning "of cows." Why it was applied to this group of plants—which also includes cranberries, bilberries, and several species of blueberries—is unclear. Although the berries are not considered edible, early settlers are reported to have boiled and sweetened them with honey to create a passable dessert. Wild birds and animals eat them without hesitation.

Squaw-huckleberry grows in open woodlands and along forest edges throughout North Carolina and Virginia and can be found in scattered locations along the Parkway. The pictured specimen was photographed at the Mahogany Rock Overlook at Mile 235.

Japanese Honeysuckle *Lonicera japonica*

Plate 76

Color: White–Yellow

Bloom: May–July

The Japanese honeysuckle is a woody, high-climbing vine that covers nearly everything it comes in contact with. Despite being a hard-to-eradicate bane to farmers and gardeners, it does have a sweet tantalizing odor and uniquely beautiful tubular flowers, which grow in pairs from the leaf axils. They are white, sometimes tinged with pink, and fade to a buffy yellow with age. Long, curved stamens project from a two-lipped, five-lobed corolla. The evergreen, ovate leaves are rounded at the base and toothed along the edges.

Very little can be said of the practical benefits of honeysuckle except that the juice of the plant is reported to relieve the pain of bee stings and that it is favored by hummingbirds. It grows in woodlands and pastures and along fencerows. The pictured specimen was photographed near the Walnut Cove View at Mile 396.4.

Hedge Bindweed *Calystegia sepium*

Plate 77

Color: White–Pink

Bloom: May–August

Hedge bindweed is a funnel-shaped, morning-glory-like flower with two heart-shaped bracts under the blossom. The flower can be pure white or pink with white vertical stripes. The 2- to 5-inch-long leaves are triangular or arrow-shaped. The twining stem is fairly smooth and grows up to 10 feet long. It is the twisting, turning stem that entangles everything in its path that is responsible for the name "bindweed." The species name, *sepium*, is from the Latin, meaning "of hedges or fences," thus describing where this species is usually found.

American Indians were said to have rubbed bindweed leaves over their bodies and then handled rattlesnakes without mishap. Early settlers used an extract from bindweed as a flavoring in a liqueur. Hedge bindweed is often called morning glory, and Henry David Thoreau wrote of it in 1854: "Well named morning glory. Its broad, bell- and trumpet-shaped flowers, faintly tinged with red, are like the dawn itself."

This is an extremely hardy plant and seems to flourish in almost any kind of soil. It is fairly common along the unmowed grassy edges of overlooks and parking areas. The pictured specimen was photographed at the Sheet's Gap Overlook at Mile 252.8.

Plate 78

New Jersey Tea *Ceanothus americanus*

Color: White

Bloom: June–September

New Jersey tea is a low-growing shrub with tiny white flowers that rise in oval clusters from the leaf axils of the current year's shoots. Each flower is about ⅕ inch across, with five white petals and five protruding stamens. The clusters measure about ½ inch across and about 1 inch long. The leaves are 1 to 3 inches long, three-veined, toothed, ovate, and sharp pointed.

The dried leaves of this nitrogen-fixing plant make an excellent tea that was very popular among the early settlers. The brew was especially favored during the period of the Revolutionary War.

New Jersey tea grows in open woods and clearings and along roadsides. The pictured specimen was photographed on the valley side of the stone wall that borders the Parkway across from the Mahogany Rock Overlook at Mile 235.

Plate 79

Meadow-sweet *Spiraea alba var. latifolia*

Color: White

Bloom: June–September

This woody shrub has a dense, pyramidal, terminal cluster of small white or pale pink flowers. Each flower measures about ¼ inch wide and consists of five petals, five sepals, and numerous stamens. The 1- to 2¾-inch-long leaves are ovate to lanceolate, coarsely toothed, and pale on the underside.

According to Henry David Thoreau, "an infusion of Meadow-sweet leaves tastes like China tea and is esteemed as a restorative tonic." It is also known by the name dead-man's-flower, because children in Newfoundland believed that if you picked the flower your father would die.

Although this species is not as spectacular as the garden-variety spiraeas, it does have distinctive brown seeds that persist after flowering.

Meadow-sweet is a mountain species that is normally found in moist areas, especially along stream banks. The pictured specimen was photographed on the bank of Little Glade Creek near the Little Glade Mill Pond Picnic Area at Mile 230.1.

Virgin's Bower *Clematis virginiana*

Plate 80

Color: White

Bloom: July–September

This member of the buttercup family is a climbing vine with white flowers that rise in numerous clusters from the leaf axils. The stamens and pistils are numerous and protrude from the center of the flower, often giving it a feathery appearance. Male flowers and female flowers (the latter with the feathery plumes) appear on separate plants. The leaves are opposite and compound, with three sharply toothed and sometimes lobed leaflets. The vine extends to about 10 feet and, using the twisting stem, entwines anything in its path.

This plant is known by several names, depending on where it is found. In Vermont it is called the Devil's Darning Needle, and in Maine it is wild hops. The origin of the name "virgin's bower" is unclear. However, in 1884 the medical journal *Lloyd's Report* stated that a tincture made from this plant's leaves and flowers was useful in reducing pains arising from irritation of the ovaries and urinary organs of women. But, then, the same report went on to say that it also reduced the pain of infected testicles and bladders of men.

This beautiful clematis trails over fences and along the

roadsides. The feathery, plumed female flowers give a showy appearance during the summer months. The pictured specimen was photographed at the Yadkin Valley Overlook at Mile 289.8.

Plate 81 **Love-vine** *Cuscuta gronovii*

Color: White

Bloom: August–October

Love-vine is a member of a group of plants known as dodder. It is a climbing, parasitic vine with dense clusters of small, white, bell-shaped flowers along an orange-yellow stem. The tubular, five-lobed flowers are about ⅛ inch long. The leaves, having been reduced to minute scales, appear nonexistent.

Like most plants, the love-vine produces seeds that germinate in the soil. However, the roots die as the plant grows, and it continues to survive by twisting around host plants and sending out suckers through which it obtains its nourishment.

Several species of dodder are found in the mountains, and they are best identified by the host plants on which they grow. This species, the love-vine, grows on a variety of plants, but the beaked dodder (*C. rostrata*) grows almost exclusively on blackberry plants.

Love-vine is most often found in moist areas. The pictured specimen was photographed along the trail to the Linn Cove Viaduct Observation Platform near the Linn Cove Information Center at Mile 304.7.

Plate 82 **Wintergreen** *Gaultheria procumbens*

Color: White

Bloom: September–November

This low, creeping plant, also known as teaberry or checkerberry, rarely reaches a height of more than 6 inches. The 1- to 2-inch-long, evergreen leaves are ovate and slightly toothed. The small, white, nodding, bell-shaped flowers appear singly or in clusters of two or three. The leaves have a definite wintergreen taste, and in the late fall the flowers give way to bright red, pulpy berries with a spicy taste.

Because this leathery, aromatic perennial has creeping, underground stems, it is usually found in small colonies. The pleasant wintergreen taste was well known to Indians and early settlers, and even today wintergreen extract is used to flavor teas, medicines, and candies.

Wintergreen is usually found in wooded areas, especially under evergreen trees. The pictured specimen was photographed at the Waterrock Knob Overlook at Mile 451.2.

Yellow Flowers

SIMPLE-SHAPED

Plate 83   **Smooth Yellow Violet** *Viola eriocarpa var. leiocarpa*
Color: Yellow
Bloom: March–May

This is one of the earliest blooming of the mountain violets. The bright yellow, dark-lined blossom precedes the leaves in pushing up through the winter debris of the forest floor. The blossom nods at the top of a smooth stem and waits for the later emerging, heart-shaped, broad, smooth leaves. The round-leaved yellow violet (*V. rotundifolia*) is a similar mountain violet but with smaller blossoms and basal leaves that are more roundish and expand with the blossoms in early spring. This species does not have stem leaves as does the smooth yellow violet.

The smooth yellow violet can be found as early as the latter part of March, amid the clutter of dead leaves along the edge of woodland trails. The pictured specimen was photographed along the trail from the parking area to the Jumpinoff Rocks Overlook at Mile 260.3.

Plate 84   **Halberd-leaved Violet** *Viola hastata*
Color: Yellow
Bloom: April–May

This pretty little yellow violet is more apt to be found along wooded trails than around open overlooks. Its lower petals show the dark streaks typical of most violets, and the backs of the petals are tinged with violet. The best identifying characteristic, however, is the leaves, which are long and arrow-shaped and exhibit distinctive dark green veins against a lighter green background. The name "halberd" refers to a fifteenth- or sixteenth-century weapon that consisted of a battle-ax and spike mounted on a long pole. The shape of the weapon vaguely resembles the shape of this violet's leaves.

Despite the fact that this violet is named for a weapon, violets in general are said to represent the more noble and peaceful of human traits. A French botanist named Gerard wrote in 1633: "The sweet violets, through their beauty of color and exquisite form, do bring to a gentle and manly mind, the remembrance of honesty, comeliness and all kinds of virtue."

The halberd-leaved violet is mainly a Northern species, which in the South is restricted to the mountains. The pictured specimen was photographed along the trail from the parking area to the Jumpinoff Rocks Overlook at Mile 260.3.

Kidneyleaf Buttercup *Ranunculus abortivus*

Plate 85

Color: Yellow

Bloom: March–June

This 6- to 24-inch-tall plant has stalked, kidney-shaped basal leaves, with toothed and wavy margins. The stem leaves are stalkless, linear, and divided into as many as three lobes. The stem is topped by small, inconspicuous yellow flowers with very small reflexed or drooping petals. Actually the kidneyleaf buttercup does not look much like a buttercup because, as its species name *abortivus* implies, the floral petals are greatly reduced in size. Another buttercup with reduced petals is the hooked buttercup (*R. recurvatus*); its petals are in fact shorter than the underlying recurved sepals. The basal leaves are roundish and deeply divided into three lobes. This species gets its name from the tiny hooked beaks on the seeds.

The kidneyleaf buttercup—known also as chicken-pepper, kidney-leaved crowfoot, and small-flowered crowfoot—was sometimes used by early settlers to brew a decoction that was consumed as a remedy for syphilis.

A number of species of buttercups are found along the Parkway, but this one is the earliest to appear. It grows in moist, shaded areas. The pictured specimen was photographed at the High Spiney Spur Overlook at Mile 218.7.

Plate 86

Common Buttercup *Ranunculus acris*

Color: Yellow

Bloom: May–August

The common buttercup is the most familiar of a number of species of buttercups found along the Parkway. It is a tall (up to 24 inches), erect, hairy, and branching plant topped with golden yellow flowers. Each flower is about 1 inch wide, with five overlapping petals backed by five spreading, green sepals. The basal leaves are deeply cut into five or seven unstalked segments. The upper leaves, similar but smaller, are scattered along the stem.

Similar species also found along the Parkway include the hispid buttercup (*R. hispidus*), which has a hairy, more erect stem, narrow petals that are spaced rather than overlapping, and leaves that are divided into only three segments; the creeping buttercup (*R. repens*), which branches from creeping runners and is best recognized by pale blotches on the leaves; and the bulbous buttercup (*R. bulbosus*), a smaller, hairy plant with flowers similar to the common buttercup but having reflexed, or drooping, sepals below the flower.

The buttercups grow in fields, open woods, moist areas, and waste places. The pictured specimen of the common buttercup was photographed at the Grandview Overlook at Mile 281.5.

Plate 87

Yellow Star-grass *Hypoxis hirsuta*

Color: Yellow

Bloom: March–June

This plant is easily recognized by its slender, 4- to 12-inch-long, hairy, grass-like leaves and bright yellow, star-like flowers. The flowers appear in loose clusters at the top of 3- to 6-inch hairy stems, and each flower is six-pointed, consisting of three petals and three petal-like sepals. Protruding from the flower's center are six quite visible stamens.

Yellow star-grass is a widespread species and can be found growing singly or in scattered colonies along the entire length of the Parkway. The pictured specimen was photographed along the trail to the Fox Hunter's Paradise Overlook at Mile 218.7.

Common Cinquefoil *Potentilla simplex* Plate 88

Color: Yellow

Bloom: April–June

At first glance, common cinquefoil is often mistaken for a yellow-flowered strawberry plant. However, like most cinquefoils, it has radial, five-lobed leaves that are responsible for the plant often being referred to as Five Fingers. The toothed leaves and the bright yellow, five-petaled flowers rise from runners on separate stalks. Dwarf cinquefoil (*P. canadensis*) is very similar, except that the lobes of the more rounded leaves are toothed only along the upper half of the margin.

The generic name, *Potentilla*, is indicative of the powers attributed to cinquefoil. It was believed, especially during the Middle Ages, to possess potent medicinal powers. A tea made from the leaves was used as a mouthwash and was said to cure inflammations of the mouth and gums. Also, a poultice made from various parts of the plant was widely used to heal skin wounds.

Because cinquefoil thrives well in poor soil, it often becomes a pest to farmers and gardeners. However, it can be eradicated by simply fertilizing the soil and letting other plants take over. This plant is common throughout the length of the Parkway and can be found blooming from April through May. The pictured specimen was photographed at the Mahogany Rock Overlook at Mile 235.

Rough-fruited Cinquefoil *Potentilla recta* Plate 89

Color: Yellow

Bloom: June–July

Of the three most common species of cinquefoil found along the Parkway, the rough-fruited cinquefoil is the largest. Both the common cinquefoil (*P. simplex*) and the dwarf cinquefoil (*P. canadensis*) are ground-hugging plants with small, bright yellow flowers. This plant, on the other hand, has erect, hairy stems growing to a height of 2 feet and relatively large (1 inch diameter), pale yellow flowers. Its leaves, five to seven narrowly oblong, coarsely toothed, finger-like leaflets, are typical of the cinquefoils. The flowers, each with five notched petals, appear in flat, terminal clusters atop the numerous stems.

This plant is a European import that in some sections of the country is becoming a rapidly spreading weed. The dark purple berries are reported to be edible, and according to the journals of Henry David Thoreau, "the berries are peculiar in that, even when red, they are nearly as pleasant-tasted as the more fully ripe dark-purple ones."

Rough-fruited cinquefoil is found around overlooks, in fields, and along the Parkway roadsides. It is especially common in mid-June along the northern section in Virginia. The pictured specimen was photographed at the Stewart Knob Overlook at Mile 110.9.

Plate 90   **Trout Lily** *Erythronium americanum*

Color: Yellow

Bloom: April–May

This handsome flower nods at the top of a 4- to 10-inch stem that rises from between two long, elliptic, mottled basal leaves. The bright yellow, lily-like flower consists of three petals and three petal-like sepals, which are all curved backward. Six stamens with dark brown anthers noticeably protrude from the flower's center.

This plant is known by several names, the most common of which is trout lily. The origin of this name is obscure, but the plant is often found growing along trout streams and it does appear at about the same time the trout fishing season begins. Another name, adder's tongue, might refer to the protruding stamens, which vaguely resemble a snake's tongue.

The trout lily is a common mountain flower usually found in moist woodlands. The pictured specimen was photographed near Rake's Mill Pond at Mile 163.

Yellow Wood Sorrel *Oxalis stricta*

Plate 91

Color: Yellow

Bloom: May–October

Yellow wood sorrel is a delicate herb with heart-shaped,
over-like leaves and bright yellow, five-petaled flowers.
e plant is no more than 6 inches in height, but it is quite
nmon and not very difficult to find.

his plant, also known as oxalis, is a popular woodland
. The stalks and leaves may be chewed directly or
l to lettuce in a salad. The word oxalis, however,
sour, and oxalic acid can be poisonous if consumed
e quantities.

leaves are sensitive to cold and will fold on cool
s a protection against the change in temperature.
ults in the plant being known also as Sleeping
Other names include sour trefoil and "bread and
What this plant is called is pretty much deter-
the area in which you find it. The pictured
was photographed near the intersection of the
nd Route 21, at Mile 229 near Sparta, North
n those parts it is called yellow wood sorrel.

AND ASTER-LIKE

Senecio spp.

Plate 92

ow

ril–July

y-blooming members of the sunflower family,
as groundsel, sport bright yellow, daisy-like
at-topped clusters. Each small flower consists
twelve yellow petals around a yellowish central
en ragwort (*S. aureus*) is the earliest bloomer and
art-shaped basal leaves and long, lanceolate,
n leaves. The roundleaf ragwort (*S. obovatus*) has
asal leaves that are wider above the middle and
a slender stalk. The stem leaves are lanceolate

and lobed. Small's ragwort (*S. smallii*) has elliptic to oblong, finely toothed, long-stalked basal leaves and lobed stem leaves.

As suggested by the Indian name "squaw-weed," ragwort was used as a remedy for a variety of female conditions. The Catawbas made a tea from all parts of the plant to alleviate the pains of childbirth.

Golden ragwort blooms from early April to June in wet meadows and damp woods. Roundleaf ragwort inhabits wooded slopes and rocky areas, and Small's ragwort blooms from May to early June in pastures and meadows and along roadsides. The pictured specimen of golden ragwort was photographed below the dripping waters of a spring near the Licklog Ridge Overlook at Mile 349.2.

Plate 93. **Hawkweed** *Hieracium spp.*

Color: Yellow

Bloom: May–July

Hawkweed is among the most common wildflowers along the Parkway and is represented by a number of similar species. Three of these, grouped by virtue of having a leafless stem, are King Devil, the mouse-ear hawkweed, and the rattlesnake-weed. King Devil (*H. pratense*), also known as field hawkweed, has a 12- to 24-inch-tall, hairy stem bearing a tight cluster of bright yellow, dandelion-like flowers. The bracts surrounding each flower are covered with dark hairs, as are the spoon-shaped basal leaves. Mouse-ear hawkweed (*H. pilosella*) has a shorter stem bearing a single, yellow, dandelion-like flower. Its small mouse-ear-like leaves form a basal rosette. The rattlesnake-weed (*H. venosum*) has a loose floral cluster, and its green basal leaves are streaked with red or purple veins, giving the appearance of a rattlesnake's skin.

Also common along the Parkway is hairy hawkweed (*H. gronovii*), which has one or more linear leaves on the lower half of its hairy stem. This species also has a relatively loose floral cluster. The panicled hawkweed (*H. paniculatum*) also has loose clusters, with the flowers on slender stalks branching horizontally from the main stem in open panicles. The slightly toothed leaves of this species ascend a hairless stem.

The pictured specimen of the mouse-ear hawkweed was photographed at Mason's Knob at Mile 126.2.

Cat's-ear *Hypochoeris radicata* Plate 94

Color: Yellow

Bloom: May–July

This plant features a tall, slender stem that might or might not be branched. Each stem, or branch, supports a single, bright yellow, dandelion-like blossom. The stems are smooth except for occasional scale-like bracts. The basal leaves range from 2 to 6 inches long and are pinnately lobed and very hairy on both sides. There are a number of plants named after various parts of a cat: cat-tail, cat-foot, and now cat's-ear, which is so named because of the hairy texture of this plant's leaves.

Without a careful examination of the leaves, this plant could easily be mistaken for a dandelion or a hawkweed. It is found in scattered locations throughout the length of the Parkway. The pictured specimen was photographed at the Raven's Fork View at Mile 469.8.

Yellow Goat's-beard *Tragopogon dubius* Plate 95

Color: Yellow

Bloom: May–July

This strikingly beautiful plant has a smooth stem bearing clasping, grass-like leaves. The stem is swollen at the top, forming an urn-shaped base for a mass of bright-yellow, dandelion-like rays. The flower head is surrounded by green, stiletto-like bracts jutting out from behind the rays.

This European import is infrequent in North Carolina, but it inhabits a number of locations along the Parkway in Virginia. The British call this plant Jack-Go-to-Bed-at-Noon, because the blossom has a tendency to spring open at first sunlight and close again around noontime. For farmers in some provinces of France, the blossom's closing announces lunchtime.

tures of this species is the bracts below the flower heads, which are sticky to the touch. The leaves are long and lanceolate with wavy and sparsely toothed edges. The lower leaves are somewhat ovate.

Also known as the silk aster, this plant grows in barren and sandy soil in fields and pastures and along roadsides. The pictured specimen was photographed at the second overlook on the road into the Linn Cove Information Center at Mile 317. Look for this flower from late July to mid-August on the opposite side of the overlook's stone wall.

Plate 103 ### Tall Sunflower *Helianthus giganteus*

Color: Yellow

Bloom: July–October

This species, one of several sunflowers found along the Parkway, has a tall, rough, reddish stem bearing from several to many bright yellow flowers. Each flower measures 1½ to 3 inches across and has ten to twenty rays surrounding a yellowish central disk. The bracts beneath the flowers are narrow, thin, and green. The leaves are 3 to 7 inches long, mostly alternate but at times opposite. They are also rough, lanceolate, finely toothed, and pointed at the tip. This plant has been known to reach a height of 12 feet. A related species, the thin-leaved sunflower (*H. decapetalus*), has larger leaves that narrow into wings along the leafstalks.

The tall sunflower is usually found in wet thickets and other damp areas. The pictured specimen was photographed along a stream near Mile 232.5.

Plate 104 ### Jerusalem Artichoke *Helianthus tuberosus*

Color: Yellow

Bloom: July–October

This large member of the sunflower family grows to a height of 10 feet. The flowers measure up to 3 inches across and consist of ten to twenty yellow rays surrounding a yellowish disk. Bracts beneath the flower heads are narrow and spreading. The ovate-to-lanceolate leaves have winged stalks and three main veins; the lower leaves are opposite, the upper ones alternate.

This large, coarse plant was an important source of food for Indians and early settlers. The edible tubers are highly nutritious; unlike potatoes, they contain no starch, but rather carbohydrates that are metabolized into natural sugar. Today Jerusalem artichoke is widely available in vegetable markets and health food stores. The tubers are delicious when boiled or baked like potatoes.

The common name, Jerusalem, is probably a corruption of the Italian word *girasole*, meaning "turning to the sun." This plant, with its flowers facing the sun, is found in thickets and on woodland borders. The pictured specimen was photographed at the Pink Beds Overlook at Mile 410.3.

Green-headed Coneflower *Rudbeckia laciniata* Plate 105

Color: Yellow

Bloom: July–October

According to some sources, this plant, also known as the tall coneflower, grows to a height of 12 feet. While this might be true, the average height of the specimens growing along the Parkway is more in the 2- to 6-foot range. In any case, it is an impressive wildflower, with its numerous, long-stalked flower heads. Each flower is 2½ to 4 inches across, with six to ten bright yellow rays and a greenish, cone-shaped central disk. The tall, branching stems are smooth and somewhat whitened. The lower leaves are stalked and usually divided into five to seven deeply cut, three-lobed leaflets, which are often as much as 12 inches wide. The upper leaves are smaller, stalkless, and divided into three or five segments.

The green-headed coneflower grows in rich, moist, open woods as well as on rocky slopes. The pictured specimen was photographed along the trail to the Linn Cove Viaduct Observation Platform near the Linn Cove Information Center at Mile 302.

Plate 106

Wing-stem *Verbesina alternifolia*

Color: Yellow

Bloom: August–September

This disheveled-looking plant has sunflower-like blossoms with ten or fewer drooping, yellow rays surrounding an untidy, mop-like disk. The rather large, oblong leaves taper at the base and flow into "wings" along the stem. The upper leaves are alternate, as suggested by the species name *alternifolia*, but the lower ones may be opposite. This is a tall plant, growing to as high as 10 feet.

Wing-stem is similar to crown-beard, which has opposite leaves and a tighter cluster of disk flowers.

Wing-stems are normally found in damp areas in alluvial woods and meadows. The pictured specimen was photographed at the Big Ridge Overlook at Mile 403.8.

Plate 107

Common Sneeze-weed *Helenium autumnale*

Color: Yellow

Bloom: September–October

The winged stems of this plant bear yellow, daisy-like flower heads with fan-shaped ray petals that droop backwards. The disk flowers form a conspicuous greenish yellow, ball-like structure resembling a pincushion at the center of the flower head. The leaves are up to 6 inches long, alternate, lanceolate, and toothed, with bases that form winged extensions down the stem.

The purple-headed sneeze-weed (*H. flexuosum*), also found along the Parkway, is similar but has a central, button-like floral disk that is deep purplish in color.

American Indians used the dry, nearly mature flower heads and the dried leaves in making a snuff, which when inhaled would cause sneezing, thus warding off evil spirits. A tea made from the leaves was used as a laxative.

Common sneeze-weed is a late summer and fall flower that is most commonly found in moist meadows and fields. The pictured specimen was photographed in a wet meadow near the intersection of the Parkway and County Road 1109 near Mile 231.8.

Squaw-root *Conopholis americana*   Plate 108

Color: Yellow–Brown

Bloom: March–June

This strange-looking, parasitic plant has yellowish flowers emerging from beneath ovate, yellowish brown scales
on a thick, fleshy stalk. The small, ½-inch-long flowers
consist of an upper lip that forms a narrow hood over a
three-lobed, spreading lower lip. Leaves are nonexistent,
being represented instead by scales.

As a parasite, squaw-root gets its nourishment from the
roots of trees, chiefly oak trees. The scaly stalks, which
resemble the cones of the white pine, often appear in large
clumps.

This plant's generic name is from two Greek words,
Conos, meaning "cone," and *pholis*, meaning "scales." As
the species name *americana* indicates, this is one of our
native American plants. No doubt at one time this plant
was used by American Indians as either a food or for medicinal purposes, perhaps for female ailments, which might
explain how the plant came to be known as squaw-root.
Early settlers probably also made use of this plant and perhaps they are responsible for its other common name,
cancer-root.

Squaw-root grows in dry woods, especially in the vicin-
ity of oak trees. The pictured specimen was photographed
along the trail to the Jumpinoff Rock Overlook at Mile
260.3.

Bellwort *Uvularia spp.*   Plate 109

Color: Yellow

Bloom: April–May

The bellworts are low woodland plants with small, yellowish, usually solitary, bell-like flowers that dangle from
the ends of branches beneath the upper leaves. The bell-

worts are early springtime bloomers, and three species can be found in the mountains.

The mountain bellwort, *U. pudica*, has a solitary dangling flower and shiny green leaves that are rounded at the base. The perfoliate bellwort, *U. perfoliata*, also has a solitary dangling flower, the interior of which is roughened with tiny orange grains, and shiny green leaves that are pierced by the stem. The large-flowered bellwort, *U. grandiflora*, usually has two or more dangling flowers, which are slightly larger than those of the mountain or perfoliate bellworts, and stem-clasping leaves that are shiny green above but whitish and downy beneath. One other species of the genus *Uvularia* that is found along the southern section of the Parkway is wild oats, *U. sessilifolia*. It is similar to the mountain bellwort except that its stem is smooth rather than downy and it is normally found in colonies rather than singly.

The bellworts have long been known by other names, such as cowbells, haybells, and strawbells. As far back as 1785, Indians and early settlers were eating the young shoots of these plants like asparagus. Also, Indians used the leaves and roots to make a salve for healing wounds and skin ulcers.

The pictured specimen of the mountain bellwort was photographed at the Cascades Overlook at Mile 272.

Plate 110 **Hop Clover** *Trifolium agrarium*

Color: Yellow

Bloom: June–September

Hop clover has small, yellowish, pea-like flowers clustered in roundish oblong heads. The leaves are divided into three wedge-shaped leaflets that are stalkless. The leaflets are oblong and measure ½ to ¾ inch long. The stems are smooth and erect.

This low-growing and spreading plant is known by several names, including yellow suckling, yellow trefoil, and shamrock. Shamrock is derived from the word *seamrog*, a diminutive of *seamar*, the Irish word for "clover." In Ireland the plant was a potent charm against witches and fairies long before it was christianized as Saint Patrick's symbol of the Trinity. Other plants that have been called shamrock and sold as such include wood sorrel, black medick, and even red and white clover.

Hop clover is often found in lawns and gardens as well as in open pastures and on rocky slopes. The pictured specimen was photographed on a rocky slope across the Parkway from the Stack Rock Overlook at Mile 304.6.

Pale Touch-me-not *Impatiens pallida*

Plate 111

Color: Yellow

Bloom: July–September

This is a smooth, branching member of the jewel-weed family, which has a translucent stem filled with a watery juice. It grows to 5 feet tall and has alternate, egg-shaped leaves with coarsely toothed edges. The odd-shaped, canary yellow flower dangles on a thread-like stalk from the leaf axils. Each flower is tubular, about ¾ inch long, and ends in a tail-like spur. Sometimes the interior of the flower is sparingly spotted with reddish brown dots. The fruit is a capsule which, when touched, explosively splits open into five spirally twisted parts, hurling the seeds in all directions. This accounts for the name "touch-me-not."

The soothing and medicinal juices of this plant have long been used as a remedy for poison ivy and other skin irritations. In the Northeast, the plant is known as silverweed, because of the silvery appearance of the leaves when placed in water.

This plant is quite common along the Parkway, especially at elevations of 2,000 to 5,000 feet. The pictured specimen was photographed at the Yadkin Valley Overlook at Mile 289.8.

Plate 112

Golden Alexander *Zizia aurea*

Color: Yellow

Bloom: April–May

Golden Alexander, a member of the parsley family, bears loose, flat-topped clusters of bright yellow flowers. The leaves are twice divided, with three to seven long, pointed, toothed leaflets.

Also known as meadow parsnip, this plant grows from a fleshy root crown or taproot. There is no evidence that the plant was ever used as a source of food or for medicinal purposes.

This plant grows in alluvial woods, swamp forests, and creek bottoms. The pictured specimen was photographed near the Short's Knob Overlook at Mile 157.6.

Plate 113

Wild Parsnip *Pastinaca sativa*

Color: Yellow

Bloom: June–July

This plant's main stem, which is stout, hollow, and ribbed, rises from a fleshy taproot to a height of 2 to 5 feet. It is topped by a loose umbrella-like cluster formed by a number of small, tight secondary clusters supported by radiating floral stalks. The pinnately divided leaves consist of five to fifteen lobed, sharply toothed, egg-shaped leaflets.

Little information is available concerning the edibility of this plant, however the fleshy taproot may have been used as a source of food by Indians and early settlers. Wild parsnip does belong to a large, widely distributed family of plants that includes a number of present-day foods such as carrots, celery, and a number of herbs. The genus name, *Pastinaca*, is from the Latin word *pastino*, meaning "to prepare the ground for the planting of the vine."

Wild parsnip is found in fields and around overlooks

along the length of the Parkway. The pictured specimen was photographed at the Lickstone Ridge Overlook at Mile 458.9.

Fringed Loosestrife *Lysimachia ciliata* Plate 114

Color: Yellow

Bloom: June–August

The erect and sometimes branched stem of this plant bears bright yellow, five-pointed flowers, which rise on stalks from the leaf axils of opposite leaves. The leafstalks are fringed with spreading hairs, thus explaining the name "fringed." Each of the flowers are about ¾ inch across, with five minutely toothed petals that come to a sharp point at the tips. The 2½- to 5-inch-long leaves are lanceolate and/or ovate. The whorled loosestrife (*L. quadrifolia*), which is quite common along several sections of the Parkway, has similar flowers and leaves in whorls of four but lacks the fringed leafstalks.

It has long been believed that this plant's genus name, *Lysimachia*, is derived from the Greek word *lusimakhos*, meaning "ending strife." It was thought that placing cuttings from this plant in the yokes of teams of oxen would lessen the strife between the animals when "under the plow." This also helps explain the common name "loosestrife." During the period of the American Revolution, colonial patriots refused to drink the tea of commerce and drank instead "Liberty Tea," made from the leaves of the loosestrifes.

This plant grows in low, moist fields and pastures as well as along streambeds. The pictured specimen was photographed near the intersection of the Parkway with Route 18 at Mile 248.1 near Laurel Springs, North Carolina.

Evening Primrose *Oenothera biennis* Plate 115

Color: Yellow

Bloom: June–October

These showy, yellow, lemon-scented flowers stand atop leafy stalks 2 to 6 feet tall. Each flower measures 1 to 2 inches across and has four bright yellow petals and an X-shaped stigma in the center. Four downward-pointing sepals surround the base of the long floral tube.

This night-flowering biennial opens in the evening, at which time its scent becomes the strongest, and closes by the following noon. This is to the advantage of the primrose, because it is pollinated by night-flying moths and insects. A similar, but day-blooming species, sundrops (*O. fruticosa*), has leaves that are lance-shaped and plain-edged and seed pods that are strongly ribbed.

The roots of the evening primrose are edible during its first year and are especially good if collected before the plant has had a chance to bloom. The roots are used in soups and stews, and the leaves can be chopped and used in salads. White-tailed deer, small rodents, birds, and caterpillars all feed on various parts of both of these species.

These plants are normally found in dry open areas. The pictured specimen was photographed at the Grandfather Mountain Overlook at Mile 307.5.

Plate 116 **Common St. John's-wort** *Hypericum perforatum*

Color: Yellow

Bloom: June–September

Common St. John's-wort is a bushy herb with bright yellow, five-petaled flowers that grow in broad, branched clusters. The flower's asymmetrical petals are marked with tiny black dots along the margins, and numerous stamens protrude from the flower's center. This is a leafy plant with many small, opposite, elliptic leaves. Holding a leaf up to the light will reveal small translucent dots.

This plant was imported from Europe and first appeared in the Klamath River section of California about the year 1900. It quickly spread and by 1951 had infested nearly 2 million acres. It was finally controlled by importing a European beetle that feeds on the plant.

This is the most common of several species of St. John's-wort in the mountains. The shrubby St. John's-wort (*H. prolificum*) is a many-branched shrub with woody, two-edged twigs crowned by a mass of flowers. The

St. Andrew's Cross (*H. stragalum*) has four narrow petals forming an oblique cross and two large sepals.

St. John's-wort is found in old fields and along roadsides. The pictured specimen of common St. John's-wort was photographed at the Big Spy Mountain Overlook at Mile 26.3.

Crown-beard *Verbesina occidentalis*

Plate 117

Color: Yellow

Bloom: August–October

Even when at its flowering peak, this tall-growing herb has a rather disheveled appearance. Its stout, branched stem supports numerous flower heads in rather loose clusters. Each flower head has two to five yellow rays set in a decidedly irregular manner around a yellowish central disk. At times, the yellow rays are partly white. The rather rough leaves are opposite, spade-shaped, 4 to 8 inches long, sawtoothed, and sharp pointed. The leafstalks are winged, with the wings extending down the plant's stem.

Crown-beard grows in open woods and fields and along roadsides. The pictured specimen was photographed at the Doughton Park Overlook near Mile 241.

ELONGATED CLUSTERS

Common Winter Cress *Barbarea vulgaris*

Plate 118

Color: Yellow

Bloom: April–August

Common winter cress is a tufted plant with somewhat elongated spikes of bright yellow flowers. Each flower has four petals that form a cross. The upper lobed leaves are stalkless and clasp the stem. The larger, lower leaves are divided into five segments, with the terminal segment being large and rounded. Early winter cress (*B. verna*) is very similar but has more segments or lobes (as many as ten pairs) on the lower leaves.

The glossy and edible young leaves of this plant are a rich source of vitamin C and were eaten by early settlers to combat scurvy. The leaves remain green through the winter, even beneath ice and snow. New leaves may appear during brief thaws. Throughout the winter they can be used raw in salads (they are as bitter as endive) or cooked like Swiss chard. However, from flowering time until killing frost, the leaves are too bitter to be palatable.

Common winter cress can be found blooming from April well into August in open fields and meadows. Sometimes they turn the fields into blankets of yellow. The pictured specimen was photographed at an unmarked overlook near Mile 204.

Plate 119

Yellow Sweet Clover *Melilotus officinalis*

Color: Yellow

Bloom: May–October

This is a loosely branched plant with long, tapering spikes of small, yellow, pea-like flowers. Each flower measures about ¼ inch long, and the clusters, which are about 6 inches long, rise from the axils of three-part leaves. Each of the three leaflets is ½ to 1 inch long, lanceolate to ovate, and shallowly toothed.

This import from Europe is also known as king's-clover, plaster-clover, and yellow melilot. The leaves, like those of the white sweet clover, have a vanilla-like odor when crushed and are often used as a flavoring. In early days in Europe, the flowers were boiled with lard and used with much success as a salve for ulcers and open sores.

Yellow sweet clover grows in open fields and waste areas and along roadsides. The pictured specimen was photographed at the Poor Mountain View at Mile 134.8.

Plate 120

Woolly Mullein *Verbascum thapsus*

Color: Yellow

Bloom: June–September

This tall, leafy plant with its club-like spike of bright yellow flowers is unmistakable. The erect, woolly stem, which is tightly packed with flowers, flower buds, and whitish woolly leaves, rises from a rosette of thick, velvety basal leaves.

Such names as Candlewick and Miner's-candle allude to past uses for this plant. Roman soldiers dipped the stalks in grease for use as torches, and to this day the leaves are used as wicks for oil lamps. Indians used the basal leaves to line their moccasins, and early settlers placed the leaves in their socks as protection against the cold. In some areas the leaves were even used as a substitute for tobacco.

Woolly mullein grows in pastures, open fields, and waste areas. The pictured specimen was photographed in an open field at Mile 267.1.

Partridge Pea *Cassia fasciculata*

Plate 121

Color: Yellow

Bloom: June–September

This 1- to 3-foot-tall plant has long, feathery, pinnately divided leaves consisting of six to fifteen pairs of small, linear-to-oblong leaflets. Each leaflet is tipped with a tiny bristle. Tucked in the leaf axils are large, yellow, five-petaled flowers that have dark anthers drooping from a reddish center. The floral petals are interesting in that they vary in size and shape.

Partridge pea is also known as the large-flowered sensitive pea because it has a gland located at the base of each leaflet that when touched causes the margins of the leaflet to curl inward. This plant grows in weedy areas and on woodland borders. The pictured specimen was photographed at the French Broad River View at Mile 393.8.

Butter-and-eggs *Linaria vulgaris*

Plate 122

Color: Yellow

Bloom: July–September

The bright yellow, snapdragon-like flowers of this plant are crowded in a club-like spike atop a leafy stem. Each flower is two-lipped, with the upper lip having two lobes and the lower lip having three. The throat is orange, and the floral tube ends in a spur. The grass-like leaves are numerous and rather uniformly distributed along the 1- to 3-foot stem.

Despite its beauty, butter-and-eggs is widely considered a troublesome weed. Once established in a pasture, it spreads rapidly and is extremely difficult to eradicate. Farmers, especially in northern climates, refer to the plant as the "Devil's flower." It thrives in waste places and along roadsides. The pictured specimen was photographed at the Greenstone Parking Area at Mile 8.8.

Plate 123

Goldenrod *Solidago spp.*

Color: Yellow

Bloom: August–Frost

Goldenrods are the most conspicuous of the fall mountain wildflowers. Nearly twenty species grow along the Parkway, and all feature clusters of tiny, golden-rayed blossoms. Identification of individual species is often a frustrating chore. However, it is fairly easy to group the various species according to the shape of floral clusters.

Some species, among them the early goldenrod (*S. juncea*) and the sweet goldenrod (*S. odora*), have spreading, plume-like clusters. Others, like the rough-leaved goldenrod (*S. patula*), have gracefully arching clusters similar to the branches of an elm tree. Species such as the showy goldenrod (*S. speciosa*) have dense, club-like clusters, and a number of species like the erect goldenrod (*S. erecta*), the downy goldenrod (*S. puberula*), and the Roan Mountain goldenrod (*S. roanensis*) have slender, wand-like clusters.

In ancient times, physicians valued the goldenrods for their supposed healing powers. In modern times, the plants were unjustly blamed for the miseries of hay fever which, in fact, are caused by ragweed.

Goldenrods often grow in large colonies, and many border the Parkway and the overlooks. The pictured specimen, a showy goldenrod, was photographed at the Ridge Junction Overlook at Mile 355.3.

Horse-balm *Collinsonia canadensis*

Plate 124

Color: Yellow

Bloom: September–October

The 1- to 3-foot-tall, square stem identifies this plant
as a member of the mint family, and the loose, branching,
pyramidal head of pale yellow, lemon-scented flowers
identifies this species. Each flower's lower lip is fringed,
and stamens and pistils project from the floral tube. Three
or more pairs of ovate to obovate, toothed leaves are distributed along the stem.

Horse-balm belongs to the genus *Collinsonia*, a group of
flowers named in honor of Peter Collinson, a London
cloth merchant and naturalist. This particular species has
long been known for its medicinal capabilities. Early
Indian tribes of the mountains of Virginia and North Carolina used the leaves to brew a tea which when taken
internally was an excellent remedy for colds and sore
throats and when rubbed on affected limbs relieved mus-
cle pains. It might also have been used to rub down the
joints and limbs of horses, thus the name horse-balm.

Horse-balm is usually found in rich, moist woods. The
pictured specimen was photographed at the Grandfather
Mountain View at Mile 306.6.

VINES AND SHRUBS

Bush-honeysuckle *Diervilla lonicera*

Plate 125

Color: Yellow

Bloom: June–August

This 4- to 5-foot-tall shrub has nearly square branchlets
that support terminal clusters of three to seven flowers,
which range in color from sulphur yellow to orange. Each
flower is about ¾ inch long and tubular, with five distinct
lobes. Usually three of the lobes are pointed forward and
two backward, but occasionally all five are folded back-

ward. The 2- to 5-inch-long leaves are opposite, stalkless, oblong to ovate, and toothed.

The genus name for this plant, *Diervilla*, honors Dr. Diereville, a seventeenth-century traveler who found the plant in Canada and carried specimens to France. The good doctor believed that gargling with a solution made from parts of this plant relieved inflammatory or ulcerated conditions of the mouth and throat.

The range of this plant along the Parkway is pretty much limited to the mountains of southwest North Carolina. It grows in woodlands and along rocky bluffs. The pictured specimen was photographed at the Pink Beds Overlook at Mile 410.3.

SIMPLE-SHAPED

Carolina Spring-beauty *Claytonia caroliniana*　　　Plate 126

Color: Pink

Bloom: March–April

The Carolina spring-beauty sports a pair of smooth, oblong leaves midway up a stem that is topped by a loose cluster of five-petaled, pink or sometimes white flowers that are streaked with dark pink veins. Spring-beauty (*C. virginica*) is a similar but more widespread species that has much narrower, lanceolate leaves.

The generic name *Claytonia* honors John Clayton (1694–1773), who was the clerk of Gloucester County, Virginia, for fifty-one years and a highly respected botanist. Early settlers discovered that the bulb-like spring-beauty roots, when boiled in salted water, were palatable and nutritious, having the flavor of chestnuts.

The pictured Carolina spring-beauty was photographed near the path of an old logging railroad across the Parkway from the Balsam Gap Overlook at Mile 359.9.

Wild Geranium *Geranium maculatum*　　　Plate 127

Color: Pink–Lavender

Bloom: April–June

Wild geranium, also known as spotted cranesbill, has loose clusters of two to five pink-to-rose-purple, four-petaled flowers, which appear at the tips of smooth branches above a pair of five-lobed leaves. Each flower is 1 to 2 inches across, with five sharply pointed sepals peeking out from behind five rounded petals. The leaves measure up to 5 inches across, are gray-green in color and are cut into three to five deep lobes, with each lobe being deeply toothed. Like other members of the cranesbill family, this plant's fruits are shaped like a crane's bill.

Wild geranium was widely used by Indians and early

settlers for medicinal purposes. The Indians used the root to cure venereal diseases, and the settlers, who called the plant alum-root because of the astringent taste of the root, used it successfully to cure influenza among children.

This plant is partial to mountain coves and alluvial woods. The pictured specimen was photographed at the Bull Run Knob Overlook at Mile 133.6.

Plate 128

Dovesfoot Cranesbill *Geranium molle*

Color: Pink

Bloom: April–July

These small (½ inch across), pinkish flowers have deeply notched petals with a dark purple vein running lengthwise through the two lobes of each petal. The stamens in the middle of the flower are crowded together, appearing as a single style or post. The leaves are deeply cut into as many as nine segments, with the tip of each segment having three or five lobes. The seedpods, perched atop reflexed stalks, have a projecting cone that resembles a crane's bill, thus the plant's name. The term "dove's foot," with some stretch of the imagination, describes the shape of the segmented leaves. The Carolina cranesbill (*G. carolinianum*) can also be found at scattered locations along the Parkway. It is similar to the dovesfoot but has wider gaps between the more narrow segments of its leaves. Also, the stalks of the seedpods are not reflexed.

Both of these plants grow in old fields and disturbed areas and should be searched for along the edges of overlooks. The pictured specimen of dovesfoot cranesbill was photographed at the Taylor's Mountain View at Mile 97.

Plate 129

Deptford Pink *Dianthus armeria*

Color: Pink

Bloom: June–September

Deptford pink is a stiffly erect, slenderly branched plant that reaches a height of about 18 inches. The finely haired stem supports pairs of narrow, lance-like leaves that measure 1 to 2 inches long. The small flowers are borne singly or in small clusters at the top of the stem. Each flower is about ½ inch across and has five pink or rose-colored petals with tiny white spots and jagged tips.

This is an old-world plant that was at one time extremely abundant in Deptford, England; hence its name. In much of England however, this flower is known as "God's Flower." Even the generic name, *Dianthus*, is from a Latin term meaning "God's flower." Other names for this plant include grass pink and wild pink. It is now widely naturalized in North America and is frequently seen in fields and along roadsides in the Blue Ridge Mountains. The pictured specimen was photographed at the Osborne Mountain Overlook at Mile 277.9.

ODD-SHAPED

Showy Orchis *Orchis spectabilis*   Plate 130
Color: Pink–White
Bloom: April–July

This beautiful and fragrant plant of the rich woods has an elongated cluster of two to fifteen deep pink and brilliant white flowers atop a stout, four- or five-angled stem. Each flower consists of a pink hood, formed by two lateral petals and three fused sepals, arched over a bright white, lower lip-petal with a long retracted spur. The stem rises from a sheath of two bright green, egg-shaped leaves.

This plant's generic name, *Orchis*, is from the Greek word for "testicles" and refers to the roundish shape of the fleshy roots. As might be imagined, the orchis plants have long been esteemed as strong aphrodisiacs, especially when consumed with wine.

The showy orchis is found in rich hardwood forests of the mountains, often along streams. The pictured specimen was photographed along a trail at the Crabtree Meadows Recreation Area at Mile 339.5.

Plate 131 **Pink Lady's Slipper** *Cypripedium acaule*

Color: Pink

Bloom: May–July

This plant, also known as pink moccasin flower, is easily identified by its inflated, heavily veined, and deeply cleft pink pouch. Greenish brown sepals and side petals extend up and out from above the pouch. The flower rises on a 6- to 12-inch stem from the junction of two strongly ribbed, ovate leaves, which are deep green above and silvery underneath.

Indian women held the blossom of this plant in high esteem as a hair decoration, and in Maine, where the plant is collected and used as a nerve sedative, it is called nerve-root. Pink lady's slippers grow in dry, acidic, pine woodlands in scattered locations along the Parkway. The pictured specimen was photographed at the Crabtree Meadows Recreation Area at Mile 339.5.

Plate 132 **Spotted Knapweed** *Centaurea maculosa*

Color: Pink

Bloom: June–September

This highly branched, wiry-stemmed member of the star-thistle family has, in fact, the appearance of a thistle. The pink-to-lavender flower heads perched at the top of the stem are composed entirely of disk flowers; there are no petals. The base of each flower head is surrounded by harsh, prickly, black-tipped bracts. The black-tipped bracts are a prominent feature of this plant and account for the name "spotted." The lower leaves are 4 to 8 inches long and are dissected into linear segments. The upper leaves are much smaller.

Spotted knapweed can be found in fields and along roadsides in late spring, summer, and well into the fall. The pictured specimen was photographed at the Upper Goose Creek Valley Overlook near Mile 89.

Wild Bergamot *Monarda fistulosa* Plate 133

Color: Pink

Bloom: June–September

The pink-to-lavender, tubular flowers of the wild bergamot grow in a dense, rounded cluster at the top of a
square stem. Each flower is about 1 inch long, with a hairy,
two-lobed upper lip and a broader three-lobed lower lip.
The bract under the flower cluster if often tinged with
pink. The leaves are about 2½ inches long, lanceolate, and
coarsely toothed.

The aromatic leaves of this plant, a member of the
horsemint family, can be used to make a mint tea, and the
strong mint flavor is quite useful as a flavoring in cooking
a variety of foods. Early settlers found it useful in relieving
stomachaches and for cooling fevers.

This plant is found in meadows and pastures, and on
wooded slopes. The pictured specimen was photographed
along the Flat Rock Trail a short distance from the parking
area at Mile 308.2.

Bull Thistle *Cirsium vulgare* Plate 134

Color: Pink

Bloom: July–September

Also known as the common thistle, this European
native is now widely naturalized in this country. It has a
stout, leafy stem that grows from 3 to 6 feet tall and has
prickly wings descending from the base of the leaves. The
leaves are green above, pale and woolly beneath, and are
cut into a number of spiny segments. This is one of the
spiniest of the thistles, so look and smell but do not touch.

The large, pink-to-purple floral disks atop the stem are
surrounded with spiny, yellow-tipped bracts. When the
flowers go to seed, bits of thistle down act as tiny para-
chutes to carry the small seeds long distances.

Bull thistles are a common sight in many of the pastures
and fields along the Parkway. The pictured specimen was
photographed along the bridle trail near the Moses Cone
Mansion and Gift Shop at Mile 294.

Plate 135   **Field Thistle** *Cirsium discolor*

Color: Pink

Bloom: August–October

The upper leaves of this thistle fold upward to embrace the 1½- to 2½-inch-wide, pink-to-lavender flower heads. Beneath the flower heads, sepal-like bracts extend out in long colorless bristles. The spiny leaves, especially the lower ones, are deeply lobed and have a whitish wool covering the underside. The tall thistle (*C. altissimum*) is similar to the field thistle in flower structure, but most of its leaves are lanceolate, tapered at each end, and not deeply lobed or incised. Both of these species have stems that are free of spines.

Thistles have never been considered of much value. However, in 1851 Henry David Thoreau made the following observation: "How many insects a single one attracts! While you sit by it, bee after bee will visit it, and busy himself probing for honey and loading himself with pollen, regardless of your overshadowing presence."

The field thistle is essentially a mountain species and is usually found in open woods, fields, and pastures, and along roadsides. The pictured specimen was photographed at the Devil's Garden Overlook at Mile 235.8.

Plate 136   **Common Burdock** *Arctium minus*

Color: Pink

Bloom: July–October

This is a large bushy plant with prickly, pink-to-purplish flower heads. Each flower head consists of numerous florets enclosed by overlapping bracts with tiny hooked spines. The ovate leaves are rather large, growing to as much as 18 inches long. The lower leaves are heart-shaped and dark green and have yellow leaf stalks.

Common burdock owes its survival to the tiny hooks on the bracts. These barbed bracts stick to animal fur and human clothing and thus quite efficiently disperse the seedpods over wide areas. The tiny hooks and the appearance of this plant give rise to several other names, including Beggar's Buttons, Beggar's Lice, and Hurr Burr.

Early pioneers made a tea from the burdock's roots to help purify the blood, and the young leaves and roots were often eaten raw. It is rumored that eating the raw stems would "stir up lust," and the plant was sometimes used as a love potion. But then, the seedpods were also, at one time, eaten to help things "stick in your mind."

Common burdock grows in dry areas and along roadsides. The pictured specimen was photographed along the bridle trail at the Moses Cone Mansion and Craft Shop at Mile 294.

Lyon's Turtlehead *Chelone lyonii*

Plate 137

Color: Pink–Purple

Bloom: July–September

This mountain wildflower is tall and erect and has pink or rose-purple, snapdragon-like flowers that resemble turtleheads. The flowers are borne in a compact cluster atop the stem or in the axils of opposite leaves. Each flower, which is about 1 inch long, has a two-lobed upper lip arching over a three-lobed lower lip. The interior of the lower lip is "bearded" with tiny, yellow hairs.

The Lyon's turtlehead, also known as the red turtlehead, is named in honor of John Lyon, an American botanist of the early nineteenth century. Indians used a strong decoction of the entire plant to treat open wounds and sores. In 1863, Dr. Francis P. Porcher, an advisor to the surgeon general of Virginia, reported that this plant was used by early medical practitioners to relieve symptoms of jaundice and hepatic disorders.

Lyon's turtlehead is found in rich woodland coves, in spruce-fir forests, and along open streams. The pictured specimen was photographed along the trail to the Linn Cove Viaduct Observation Platform near the Linn Cove Information Center at Mile 304.7.

Plate 138 **Purple Dead Nettle** *Lamium purpureum*

Color: Pink–Purple

Bloom: March–May

Purple dead nettle is a stubby-looking plant crowded with drooping, heart-shaped leaves, which tend to overlap. The upper leaves are often purplish and the small pinkish flowers, which emerge from the leaf axils, are two-lipped, with the lower lip having two lobes.

This plant, one of the earliest blooming mountain flowers, is known as "dead" nettle because its stem lacks the bristly, stinging hairs of "real" nettles of the genus *Urtica*, such as the stinging nettle, which is quite rare along the Parkway.

Purple dead nettle is widely scattered along the Parkway in fields, along roadsides, and in other disturbed areas. The pictured specimen was photographed at the Stony Fork Valley Overlook at Mile 277.3.

Plate 139 **Henbit** *Lamium amplexicaule*

Color: Pink–Blue

Bloom: March–June

The pink-to-blue, monk's-hood-shaped flowers of this plant are grouped in whorls around the square stem and in the axils of the upper leaves. The flowers are two-lipped, with the upper lip arching over the lower lip, which is marked with a dark purple spot. The leaves are rounded and scalloped, the lower ones being long-stalked and the upper ones partly clasping the stem.

The species name for this plant, *amplexicaule*, is from the Latin term meaning "clasping" and describes the clasping leaves. The common name, henbit, probably came from old-time settlers, whose barnyard chickens fed on the seeds.

This 2- to 12-inch-tall plant is an early spring bloomer

in fields, along roadsides, and in grassy areas along many sections of the Parkway. The pictured specimen was photographed at the Smart View Overlook at Mile 154.1.

Honesty *Lunaria annua*

Plate 140

Color: Pink

Bloom: May–June

Honesty, often known as lunaria, is definitely not a run-of-the-mill mountain wildflower. This plant is one of two species of the genus *Lunaria* that were imported from Europe, where it is cultivated for its lustrous, flat, oval seedpods, which are used in dry floral bouquets. The pink, four-petaled flowers are clustered atop a hairy stem. The leaves, either opposite or alternate, are arrowhead-shaped and sharply toothed. The generic name *Lunaria* refers to the membranous, moon-like seedpods; the species name *annua* indicates that the plant blooms annually.

It is the shape of the highly prized, half-dollar-size seedpods that is responsible for a number of names for this plant, including money-plant and penny-flower. Reference materials are unclear as to why the plant is known as Honesty.

Because this plant is a relatively recent "escapee" from cultivation, it is found in only a few isolated spots along the Parkway. The pictured specimen was photographed at the Stewart Knob Overlook at Mile 110.9.

Dame's Rocket *Hesperis matronalis*

Plate 141

Color: Pink

Bloom: May–June

Dame's rocket is a onetime domestic species that has escaped from the gardens to the roadsides. Its pink-to-pale-lavender, four-petaled flowers form a loose cluster atop a 2- to 3-foot stem. The upper leaves are ovate and toothed with very short leafstalks, while the lower ones are oblong with longer leafstalks. The long, slender, erect seedpods are typical of the mustard family to which this plant belongs.

Dame's rockets are normally found in rich, moist woodland soils and along woodland borders. Along the Parkway, its range is limited to a few counties in North Carolina. The pictured specimen was photographed at the Moses Cone Manor and Craft Shop at Mile 294.

Plate 142

Goat's Rue *Tephrosia virginiana*

Color: Pink–Yellow

Bloom: May–August

Goat's rue has bicolored, pea-like flowers that vary in color from pink and white to pink and yellow. The numerous flowers are arranged in a terminal, 3-inch-wide cluster at the end of a hairy stem. The compound leaves are divided into fourteen to twenty-eight narrowly oblong leaflets. The roots are long and stringy, giving cause for this plant being referred to as Devil's Shoestrings.

Goat's rue was once routinely fed to goats to improve milk production. However, since it contains rotenone (now used as an insecticide), the practice has been discontinued. Indians used a decoction of the roots to treat intestinal worms, bladder trouble, and chronic coughing. Indian women used the plant as a shampoo to prevent thinning hair. The seeds are eaten by many birds and are especially esteemed by wild turkeys.

This plant grows in open fields and pastures along the Parkway. The pictured specimen was photographed on a rocky slope across the Parkway from the Stack Rock Parking Area near Mile 304.6.

Plate 143

Crown Vetch *Coronilla varia*

Color: Pink–White

Bloom: June–August

The pink and white, pea-like flowers of this plant arise from the leaf axils on upward curving stalks. The upper petals of each flower are pink, while the side, wing-like petals are white. The compound leaves are 2 to 4 inches long and consist of fifteen to twenty-five ovate, $1/2$- to $3/4$-inch leaflets.

Although this is a native wildflower of Europe, it can now be found throughout North America. Vetch is widely used as a ground cover and for soil improvement. It is often sown in orchards to improve the quality of the soil. A bacterium that grows on the roots of vetch, as well as most other members of the pea family, can change free nitrogen into a usable form and actually introduce nitrogen into the soil. Because the seedpods of this plant are shaped somewhat like axheads, it is often called axseed.

Crown vetch can be found growing along roadsides, in pastures, and along woodland borders. The pictured specimen was photographed near the intersection of the Parkway and Route 321 near Mile 292.

Common Milkweed *Asclepias syriaca*

Plate 144

Color: Pink

Bloom: June–August

The common milkweed is a stout plant that grows to a height of up to 5 feet. The domed, often drooping, flower clusters emerge from the upper leaf axils and vary in color from subtle shades of pink to lavender to a dull, brownish purple. The 3- to 8-inch leaves are oblong, more or less rounded at both ends, and abruptly pointed at the tip. The rather large, oblong-shaped seedpods are conspicuous in the fall after the flowers and leaves have dropped off the stem. When dry, the pods will suddenly burst open, shooting forth hundreds of silken, parachute-like seeds.

The generic name *Asclepias* comes from the Greek god of medicine, whose Latin name was Aesculapius. Although today no medicinal value is attributed to this plant, the root at one time was used extensively as a healing herb. Indians used the white sap to eliminate warts, and the root was chewed to cure dysentery. Also, the dried leaves were mixed with tobacco and smoked in a pipe to ease the symptoms of asthma. Many insects — including butterflies, bees, wasps, and beetles — feed on the milkweed blossoms.

Common milkweed can be found in almost any open field or pasture along the Parkway. The pictured specimen was photographed at the Bluff Mountain Overlook at Mile 243.4.

Plate 145 **Spreading Dogbane** *Apocynum androsaemifolium*

Color: Pink

Bloom: June–August

This 1- to 2-foot-tall shrubby plant has ascending pairs of oblong to ovate, dark green, untoothed leaves that are often drooping on short slender leafstalks. The flowers rise from the leaf axils on slender curved floral stalks and dangle like pink bells. The five lobes of each flower flare outward and the tips curve backward, thus giving this plant the name "spreading." The name "dogbane" arises from the belief that the plant was poisonous to dogs. In fact, the genus name *Apocynum* is derived from the Greek terms *apo*, meaning "away," and *kuon*, meaning "dog."

Dogbane belongs to the same family of plants as the milkweeds, so it is no surprise that the broken stem and leaves of dogbane exude a milky fluid.

Spreading dogbane grows in open woods, in meadows, and along roadsides in the mountains. The pictured specimen was photographed at the Deerlick Gap Overlook at Mile 337.2.

Plate 146 **Arrow-leaved Tearthumb** *Polygonum sagittatum*

Color: Pink

Bloom: June–Frost

The arrow-leaved tearthumb belongs to a large grouping of plants known as knotweeds or smartweeds. This species is a small, easily overlooked plant with a terminal cluster of blossoms that look more like tiny pink capsules than flowers. The slender, angular, vine-like stem is covered with sharp, recurved bristles. The leaves are shaped like arrowheads and the underside of the midrib of each leaf is lined with bristles. The lower leaves are stalked, but the upper ones clasp the stem.

This plant's unusual name, tearthumb, is usually pronounced with "tear" sounding as it does in "tear drop."

The correct pronunciation, however, is "tear," synonymous with "lacerate," which is exactly what would happen to your thumb if you pulled it along the sharp, recurved bristles of the stem.

Arrow-leaved tearthumbs thrive in wet ground, especially along streambeds or in brackish areas. The pictured specimen was photographed at the Little Glade Mill Pond Picnic Area at Mile 230.1.

Wild Basil *Satureja vulgaris* Plate 147

Color: Pink

Bloom: July–September

Wild basil is an herb with erect, spreading stems covered with soft bristles. The paired leaves are ovate, with shallowly toothed edges and a rounded base. The flowers are in a dense, rounded cluster at the top of the stem and in smaller clusters in the upper leaf axils. Each of the small flowers is tubular and two-lipped and has hairy sepals that give the clusters a woolly appearance.

This plant was probably introduced from Europe, where it is widespread. The leaves can be used as a seasoning, although they are milder than those of the commercial basil. Basil no doubt got its name from the Greek word *basilikos*, meaning "royal," because the smell is so excellent it is fit for a king's palace. It is found in pastures and open deciduous woods along the length of the Parkway. The pictured specimen was photographed at the Sheet's Gap Overlook at Mile 252.8.

New York Ironweed *Vernonia noveboracensis* Plate 148

Color: Pink–Purple

Bloom: July–September

This tall, erect plant has a smooth stem that branches upward bearing a cluster of flower heads that range in color from pink to deep purple. The 3- to 4-inch-wide clusters form loose sprays. Each flower head consists of thirty or more five-lobed disk flowers, each having a ring of purple bristles at the base of a corolla tube. Ray petals are absent. Bracts surrounding the floral heads have long hair-like tips. The leaves are from 3 to 10 inches long, lanceolate, and finely toothed.

Also known as bluetop-stickweed, this plant has been used for medicinal purposes by Indian tribes as well as early settlers. A tea made from the boiled roots was thought to relieve the symptoms of pneumonia, and in some areas the root was used as a remedy for snakebite.

New York ironweed has a preference for moist areas and is usually found along streams or in low moist meadows. The pictured specimen was photographed near the intersection of the Parkway and County Road 1109 near Mile 231.8.

Plate 149 | **Joe-pye-weed** *Eupatorium spp.*

Color: Pink–Purple

Bloom: July–October

The Joe-pye-weeds are regal plants, standing tall and proud in the meadows and thickets bordering the Parkway. So impressive is their stature that they are often referred to as queen-of-the-meadow.

Three species of Joe-pye-weed occur along the Parkway, and all feature a large pinkish-to-purplish cluster of fuzzy flowers atop a sturdy, 2- to 10-foot-tall stem. The leaves, up to 8 inches long, are thick, lanceolate, and coarsely toothed and appear in whorls around the stem.

The hollow Joe-pye-weed (*E. fistulosum*) is identified by its hollow stem and whorls of five or more leaves. The spotted Joe-pye-weed (*E. maculatum*) has a deep purple or purple-spotted stem and whorls of four or five leaves. Sweet Joe-pye-weed (*E. purpureum*) has a green stem that turns to purple at the leaf joints and whorls of three or four leaves.

According to folklore, Joe Pye was an Indian medicine man in colonial New England, who gained fame by "curing" typhoid fever and other diseases with a concoction made from these plants. The generic name *Eupatorium* refers to the Persian general Eupator, who defeated the Romans using the magical powers of these plants.

The pictured specimen of hollow Joe-pye-weed was photographed at the Little Glade Mill Pond Picnic Area at Mile 230.1.

ELONGATED CLUSTERS

Hedge-nettle *Stachys latidens*   Plate 150

Color: Pink

Bloom: June–August

This is a sturdy plant with hooded, rose pink flowers that rise in interrupted whorls near the top of a sturdy stem. Each flower has two lips. The upper lip forms a "hood" above a drooping, three-lobed lower lip. Four stamens are arched, partially hidden, beneath the hood. The paired leaves are up to 7 inches long, elliptic to lanceolate, and coarsely and sharply toothed. The species name *latidens* translates to "with broad teeth."

Hedge-nettle is primarily a mountain wildflower, and two similar, difficult-to-distinguish species grow along the Parkway. This species, *S. latidens*, is found throughout the Blue Ridge range. A very similar species, Clingman's hedge-nettle (*S. clingmanii*), is found at higher altitudes in a few southwestern North Carolina counties. The species name *clingmanii* refers to Clingman's Dome on the North Carolina–Tennessee line in the Great Smoky Mountains National Park, where the flower was first discovered.

Hedge-nettle normally inhabits moist meadows and roadsides. The pictured specimen was photographed at the Green Knob Overlook at Mile 350.4.

Hoary Tick-trefoil *Desmodium canescens*   Plate 151

Color: Pink

Bloom: June–August

The purple or pinkish, two-lobed flowers of this plant occur in loose, spike-like clusters along slender stems that branch from the upper leaf axils. Each leaf consists of three ovate, untoothed leaflets that taper to a blunted point. The stems of this particular species are covered with fine hairs. The flattened seedpods, which form a jointed, in-line cluster, resemble and stick to clothing with the tenacity of a tick.

The generic name *Desmodium*, from the Greek word *desmos*, meaning "chain," describes the plant's jointed seedpods. In 1856, Thoreau described this as an insignificant plant "lying in wait, as it were, to catch on to the hem of the berry-picker's garments and so get a lift to new quarters."

The hoary tick-trefoil, chiefly a mountain species, grows in open woods, thickets, and woodland borders. The pictured specimen was photographed at the Cahas Mountain View at Mile 139.

Plate 152 **Long-bristled Smartweed** *Polygonum cespitosum*

Color: Pink

Bloom: June–Frost

Smartweeds are easily recognized by swollen leaf joints that are wrapped in a film-like sheath. Several species occur in the mountains, and most have lance-like leaves and tiny, pink or white flowers arranged in tight terminal clusters.

The long-bristled smartweed is best recognized by the relatively long (½ inch) bristles radiating from the leaf-joint sheaths and by floral spikes that are narrower than those of other species (about ¼ inch wide). Lady's-thumb smartweed (*P. persicaria*) is a similar species that has broader floral spikes and a dark triangular blotch (the lady's thumbprint) near the base of the leaves. *Polygonum*, the generic name for this group of plants, which includes both the knotweeds and the smartweeds, is derived from the Greek words meaning "many knees," referring to the swollen leaf joints. Polygonums were an important food source for Indians and early settlers. The roots were eaten raw or cooked, the leaves were used as a seasoning, and the dried seeds were ground into flour.

The long-bristled smartweed usually inhabits moist

areas, especially along woodland borders. The pictured specimen was photographed at the Round Meadow Overlook at Mile 179.3.

Wandlike Bush-Clover *Lespedeza intermedia*

Plate 153

Color: Pink

Bloom: August–October

The typically clover-like, three-part leaves of this plant are crowded along an erect, 1- to 3-foot stem in wand-like fashion. Each leaf consists of three small, oblong-to-ovate leaflets. The small, pink-to-purple, pea-like flowers appear in short clusters in the upper leaf axils. Overall, the plant looks like a long, slender, green wand dotted with pink or purple. A very similar plant, the slender bush-clover (*L. virginica*), is also found along the Parkway. It is also a tall, erect plant with crowded leaves, but its leaflets are narrow rather than oblong or ovate.

Like most clovers, these plants are high in nitrogen and are useful in improving the soil conditions of dry areas. Also, the seeds provide food for many birds, including quail and grouse. The bush-clovers grow in fields, along roadsides, and in open woods. The pictured specimen of the wandlike bush-clover was photographed at the Osborne Mountain View at Mile 277.9.

VINES AND SHRUBS

Pinxter-flower *Rhododendron nudiflorum*

Plate 154

Color: Pink

Bloom: April–May

This plant, known also as the wild azalea, is the Parkway's earliest blooming azalea. The pink, tubular, urn-shaped flowers begin to appear in terminal clusters from mid- to late April. These attractive, early-season blooms feature five long and curved stamens protruding from the center of the flower. The leaves, which measure 2 to 4 inches long, are thin, oblong, pointed at both ends, and clustered in pseudo-whorls near the ends of the branches.

This showy, slightly fragrant shrub appears in deciduous woods, along streams, and in damp areas. The pictured specimen was photographed at Mile 219.

Plate 155 **Rhododendron** *Rhododendron spp.*

Color: Pink–Purple

Bloom: April–July

The name translates as "rose-tree," and no other plant lends itself to shaping the character and beauty of the mountain landscape as does the group known as rhododendron. Several species grace the Parkway scenery with large flower clusters and evergreen leaves. Without a doubt the most visible is the one known as great laurel.

The great laurel or rosebay (*R. maximum*) is found mostly at elevations below 3,000 feet. It grows to a height of 35 feet, and its interlocking branches often form impassable thickets. Its pinkish white, cup-like flowers appear in large clusters during June and July, and its large, leathery, oblong, evergreen leaves, which terminate in sharp angles at both ends, add year-round color to the mountain landscape.

Mountain rosebay or purple laurel (*R. catawbiense*) is normally found at elevations above 3,000 feet, and its deep-pink to purplish flowers appear from April to June. Its leaves are smaller than those of the great laurel and are rounded at both ends. This species rarely reaches a height of more than 12 feet and is found on rocky slopes, ridges, and balds.

A third species, the Carolina rhododendron (*R. minus*), is similar to the great laurel but has thinner leaves that are heavily spotted with brown below. It is usually found along streams and on wooded slopes.

The pictured specimen of great laurel was photographed near the Little Glade Mill Pond at Mile 230.1.

Trailing Arbutus *Epigaea repens*

Plate 156

Color: Pink

Bloom: April–June

Trailing arbutus is a low-growing, creeping shrub with oval, leathery, evergreen leaves that have a heart-shaped base. The pinkish-to-white flowers grow in small clusters at the ends of woody branches. Each flower consists of a floral tube that flares to form five petal-like lobes.

Much sought after because of its exquisite fragrance, this plant is also called mayflower. Legend has it that it was the first wildflower seen by the Pilgrims as they landed at Plymouth Rock, so they named it after their ship. This is an extremely sensitive plant that reacts quickly to any changes in its habitat, which might account for its scarcity.

Trailing arbutus is found in sandy and rocky woodlands throughout the mountains. The pictured specimen was photographed along the trail to the Flat Rock Overlook at Mile 308.2.

Swamp Rose *Rosa palustris*

Plate 157

Color: Pink

Bloom: May–July

This attractive but thorny plant is nearly always found near water. Its handsome flowers feature five bright pink petals surrounding a circular, yellowish central disk. The compound leaves consist of five to nine elliptic, finely toothed leaflets. The smooth, woody stems are equipped with sharp, slightly curved thorns. An important feature of this plant is the very narrow winged formations at the base of the leafstalks.

The wild or Carolina rose (*R. Carolina*) is very similar to the swamp rose and is also found at various sites along the Parkway. It is a lower growing plant of pastures and fields, with slender stems and straight, slender thorns.

This plant's species name, *pulustris*, translates to "of swamps" and aptly describes the environment in which it grows. The pictured specimen was photographed where the mill pond empties into Little Glade Creek at the Little Glade Mill Pond Picnic Area at Mile 230.1.

Plate 158 **Everlasting Pea** *Lathyrus latifolius*

Color: Pink

Bloom: May–September

The everlasting pea is a sprawling, climbing plant with clusters of large, multicolored, pea-like flowers, each flower a blend of pink, blue, and white. Pairs of narrow leaves are accompanied by well-developed tendrils, and the stems are noticeably winged.

This plant, which belongs to the genus *Lathyrus*, the Greek word for "pea," is closely related to the popular garden flower, the sweet pea. Also, like other species of *Lathyrus*, it is widely cultivated for animal fodder.

Everlasting pea can be found in old fields and waste areas throughout the length of the Parkway. The pictured specimen was photographed at the Mill Mountain View on the Roanoke Mountain Loop Road at Mile 120.3.

Plate 159 **Purple-flowering Raspberry** *Rubus odoratus*

Color: Pink–Purple

Bloom: June–August

This shrub, with maple-like leaves and rose-like flowers, is related to the fruit-producing raspberry we know so well. The flower has five pink-to-purple petals surrounding a central, circular disk of stamens and pistils. The sepals behind the petals are curiously long and finger-like. The plant is thornless, but new growth is covered with bristly hairs. The large, three- to five-lobed leaves are rounded and heart-shaped at the base.

Purple-flowering raspberry was widely used by Indian tribes, especially the Cherokees. The root was chewed to relieve coughs, the leaves produced an astringent for washing wounds and open sores, and a "tea" made from all parts of the plant was drunk as a tonic for toothaches and boils. The fruit, though somewhat bitter, was used as food.

This plant grows along woodland borders, fencerows, and thickets in the mountains. The pictured specimen was photographed at Chestoa View at Mile 320.8.

Common Morning Glory *Ipomoea purpurea*

Plate 160

Color: Pink

Bloom: July–September

This is a fast-growing vine that will coil itself around any object in its path. The large, trumpet-like flowers are usually pinkish, but may range in color from deep purple to white. Loose clusters of the flowers rise from leaf axils along the stem. The 2- to 5-inch-long leaves are broad and heart-shaped. The smooth stem can reach a length of 10 feet or more.

The morning glory is essentially a tropical or subtropical plant. The common morning glory was originally introduced into North American gardens as an ornamental, but it soon escaped cultivation, became naturalized, and is now widely considered a pesky weed. It grows in cultivated fields, along roadsides, and along fence lines. The pictured specimen was photographed at the Stewart Knob View at Mile 110.9.

Wild Bean *Phaseolus polystachios*

Plate 161

Color: Pink

Bloom: July–September

The wild bean is a trailing vine that, much like the common morning glory, will wrap itself around any stem or twig in its path. The leaves are divided into three ovate leaflets. The side leaves are egg-shaped and the center leaf is shaped like the ace of spades. The small, pink, pea-like flowers are arranged in loose, elongated clusters along thin stalks rising from the leaf axils.

Many of the bean-producing plants were important sources of food among the Indians. In autumn and early winter, women would rob the nests of small rodents, securing large piles of stored seeds. Some tribes, when taking seeds from the nests of animals, would leave corn or other food in exchange.

Wild beans grow in woods and thickets, especially in damp areas. The pictured specimen was photographed at Rakes Mill Pond at Mile 162.4.

SIMPLE-SHAPED

Common Blue Violet *Viola papilionacea*

Plate 162

Color: Blue

Bloom: March–July

This is a low-growing plant with flower heads and leaves on separate stalks. The flowers are about ¾ inch across and usually blue, although the color may range from blue to white or white with purple veins. The lower and the longest of the flower's five petals is spurred, while the two side petals are somewhat bearded. The two upper petals often curve backward. The leaves measure up to 5 inches wide, are heart-shaped, and have scalloped margins.

A similar species, the bird-foot violet (*V. pedata*), is also found in scattered localities along the Parkway. Its color is a paler blue, but it is best identified by its leaves, which are divided into many narrow segments, thus resembling a bird's foot.

Violet leaves are high in vitamin A and C and are often used in salads or cooked as greens. In some areas, this species of violet is known as Chicken Fight. Violets were used in boy's "chicken fight" games in which the spur under the curved stem is hooked with that of another's and pulled until the loser's violet is decapitated.

The common blue violet is found in moist meadows and in grassy areas along roadsides. The pictured specimen was photographed in the Peaks of Otter Park at Mile 89.

Field Pansy *Viola rafinesquii*

Plate 163

Color: Blue–White

Bloom: March–May

This delicate, pale-blue-to-white flower nods proudly atop a leafy stem. The lower and side petals are normally stained with streaks of purple, while the upper petals often fold back like a pair of wings. A bright yellow center adds a glow to the flower's charm. The branching stems support a profusion of small leaves, some lobed, some deeply divided, some spade-like.

The common name "pansy" comes from the French word *pensée*, which means "thought." In other regions however, this flower may be called Bird's Eye, Cupid's Delight, or Run-About.

The field pansy is but one of numerous species of violets found along the Parkway, and it usually inhabits fields, pastures, and roadsides. The pictured specimen was photographed on a sun-drenched embankment across the Parkway from the Short's Knob Overlook at Mile 157.6.

Plate 164

Bird's-eye Speedwell *Veronica persica*

Color: Blue

Bloom: March–June

These low, fast-growing runners have spreading, hairy stems that reach a length of up to 14 inches. The leaves are deep green, oval, toothed, and scattered along the stem. The bird's-eye-like flowers are blue with dark lines and pale centers. Note the bottom petal, which is paler and smaller than the others; this is typical of the speedwells. The common speedwell, *V. officinalis*, also found along the Parkway, is similar to the bird's-eye speedwell except that the base of the ovate leaves tapers into definite leafstalks.

How this imported plant got its name is unclear. English peasants brewed the leaves into an expectorant for treating coughs and congestion and called it "spit-well." That name could well have evolved into the term "speedwell."

This species grows in lawns, fields, and waste areas chiefly in the mountains. The pictured specimen was photographed at the Stewart Knob Overlook at Mile 110.9.

Plate 165

Periwinkle *Vinca minor*

Color: Blue

Bloom: April–May

Periwinkle grows from spreading, creeping stems, often forming large colonies. The 1-inch-wide, funnel-shaped flower has five flaring, blue-violet petals and a central depression with a whitish, star-like outline. The glossy, elliptic, 1½-inch-long leaves are paired along the stem.

The generic name *Vinca* was derived from the Latin term *vincio*, meaning "to bind," probably because the long shoots were used to bind floral wreaths. Italians call this plant *pervinca*, the French *pervenche*, and the English periwinkle. Periwinkle has had a long-standing reputation as a healing herb. A tea made from the leaves was useful in curing dysentery and was also reported to have excellent aphrodisiac effects. In 1694, Sir John Pechy, an English herbalist, wrote, "Venus owns this herb, and saith that the leaves eaten by man and his wife together, causes love between them."

Often known as myrtle, this plant escaped cultivation many years ago and now grows wild in a number of locations along the Parkway. The pictured specimen was photographed at the edge of Abbott Lake near the Peaks of Otter Lodge at Mile 86.

Bluets *Houstonia caerulea*

Plate 166

Color: Blue

Bloom: April–July

This lovely and delicate little plant is often found growing in large patches early in the spring. Often called Innocence or Quakerladies, its thread-like, tufted stem grows to a height of 3 to 6 inches. Its narrow, lower leaves form a basal rosette, and pairs of smaller leaves appear along the stem. The flower's four pale-blue-to-whitish petals surround a bright yellow "eye."

The bluet's generic name *Houstonia* honors Dr. William Houston, a Scottish physician and botanist who traveled extensively as a ship's surgeon in the 1730s and collected plants in Mexico and the West Indies. The species name *caerulea* is from the Latin word for "blue."

Bluets can be found in deciduous woodlands, meadows, and clearings. The pictured specimen was photographed along a trail near the Cumberland Knob Visitor Center at Mile 217.5.

Plate 167 **Large Houstonia** *Houstonia purpurea*

Color: Blue–White

Bloom: May–July

This 4- to 18-inch-tall plant belongs to the same family as and has many of the characteristics of the bluets. The small, four-petaled, tubular flowers range in color from deep blue to white but are usually a pale blue. They occur in broad terminal clusters above ovate-to-elliptic, paired leaves that are noticeably three-veined. The stem is erect and square.

Another species of the genus *Houstonia*, the slender-leaved houstonia (*H. tenuifolia*) can be found near the northern and southern ends of the Parkway. The flower is similar to that of the large houstonia, but the plant is profusely branched and erect, with slender, weakly angled stems and paired, linear leaves. Look for it during June near the James River Visitor Center at Mile 63.3 or during August near the Courthouse Valley View at Mile 423.5.

The large houstonia grows in deciduous forests, slopes, and clearings and along roadsides in the mountains. The pictured specimen was photographed at the Osborne Mountain View at Mile 277.9.

Plate 168 **Blue-eyed Grass** *Sisyrinchium angustifolium*

Color: Blue

Bloom: May–July

Blue-eyed grass is a stiff, grass-like plant common to meadows and grassy hillsides. The petite blue flower, which blooms atop a long flat stem, is about ½ inch across and consists of three petals and three petal-like sepals. The petals and sepals surround a yellow central disk and are each tipped with a thorn-like point. The grassy leaves are up to 20 inches long and only about ¼ inch wide, and though the plant resembles a grass, the flowers themselves have all the features of the iris family to which this plant belongs.

Blue-eyed grass can be found blooming from early May

until late July. The pictured specimen was photographed at the intersection of the Parkway and Route 21 near Mile 230.

Horse-nettle *Solanum carolinense*

Plate 169

Color: Blue–White

Bloom: June–September

Though this is a rather ugly-looking little plant, it does have an attractive pale-blue-to-white flower with a conspicuously protruding yellow center. The 3- to 5-inch-long leaves are elliptic, rough, coarsely lobed, and covered with prickles. The stems are covered with rough thorns.

This noxious weed, known also as Sandbrier, Bull Nettle, Apple-of-Sodom, and Tread Softly, belongs to the nightshade family, whose members, like horse-nettle, are often armed with thorns and spines. In times past it has been used in the treatment of epilepsy and recommended as a remedy for asthma, bronchitis, and other convulsive disorders. It grows in sandy soil, in waste areas, and along roadsides. The pictured specimen was photographed at the Basin Cove Overlook at Mile 244.7.

Spiderwort *Tradescantia subaspera*

Plate 170

Color: Blue

Bloom: June–August

The spiderwort's violet-blue flowers, with their showy yellow stamens, appear in terminal clusters above a pair of long, narrow, leaf-like bracts. Each flower is 1 to 2 inches wide with three violet-blue petals and three hairy, green sepals. The linear leaves are up to 15 inches long and come to a sharp point at the tips. At times, the leaves gently fold lengthwise, forming a long channel.

The showy spiderwort is so named because the angular arrangement of the leaves make it look like a squatting spider. Another version of the name's source suggests that the plant could supposedly cure the bite of the phalangium spider. The question is academic, however, because the phalangium spider is quite harmless.

Due to the action of enzymes within this plant, the dead blossoms do not shrivel and fall off but instead turn into runny blobs. This gives rise to another of this plant's common names, Widow Tears.

Recent research has found that the spiderwort is particularly sensitive to pollution and will change its blossom color from blue to pink within two weeks after having been exposed to severe levels of pollution. Thus, it serves as an inexpensive and accurate pollution detection device. The pictured specimen was photographed along the bridle trail at the Moses Cone Mansion and Craft Shop near Mile 294.

Plate 171 **Chicory** *Cichorium intybus*

Color: Blue

Bloom: June–Frost

The blue, stalkless flowers of this species hug a rigid, nearly leafless stem that grows as high as 4 feet tall. The clear blue flower rays are square-tipped and fringed. The basal leaves are 3 to 6 inches long and dandelion-like and have usually withered by flowering time. The stem leaves, when present, are much reduced and lanceolate and clasp the stem.

Only a few of this plant's blooms are open at any one time, and each lasts but one day. In many areas, chicory is cultivated for its roots, which are roasted and ground as a substitute for coffee. The young roots and leaves are sometimes boiled and eaten. In other areas, chicory is nothing more than a pesky weed. It grows in old fields, in waste areas, and along roadsides. The pictured specimen was photographed at Explore Park at Mile 115.

DAISY AND ASTER-LIKE

Blue-flowered Aster *Aster spp.*

Plate 172

Color: Blue–Violet

Bloom: August–Frost

Asters are among the showiest of the fall wildflowers.
Nearly twenty species have been identified in the mountains and more than half range in color from pale blue to
violet. Typically, the aster blossom consists of many (up to
100) rays surrounding a yellow disk. Normally the asters
grow to a height of 1 to 3 feet, but some may grow to
7 feet. The flowers are arranged in loose clusters of three
to thirty or more. The differences in the species are usually in the shape or structure of the leaves, and positive
identification is often difficult, even for botanists.

Asters are often referred to as "Christmas Daisies"
because they bloom so late in the year. The generic name
Aster comes from the Latin and Greek words for "star."
According to Greek legend, the aster was created out of
stardust when the god Virgo cried while looking down on
earth from the heavens.

The species most frequently encountered along the
Parkway include the Curtis's aster (*A. curtisii*), the heart-
leaved aster (*A. cordifolius*), the purple-stemmed aster
(*A. puniceus*), and the late purple aster (*A. patens*). Asters
normally grow in open woodlands, in clearings, or along
streams. The pictured purple-stemmed aster was photographed at the Little Glade Mill Pond Picnic Area at
Mile 230.1.

ODD-SHAPED

Plate 173
Crested Dwarf Iris *Iris cristata*

Color: Blue

Bloom: April–May

This single, violet-blue flower with six spreading
petal-like parts is perched atop a short slender stem.
The three downward-curving, white, purple-lined sepals
are bearded, or crested, with a yellowish orange ridge.
The 4- to 7-inch-long leaves are flat and lanceolate and
sheath the stem.

The roots of this plant can be chewed with remarkable
results. At first the taste is pleasant and sweet, but within a
few minutes, it changes to a sharp burning sensation.
Despite these strange characteristics, however, old-time
Virginia woodsmen would frequently chew the roots to
alleviate thirst.

The dwarf iris (*I. verna*) also appears in scattered areas
along the Parkway. It is similar to *I. cristata* but has leaves
that are much narrower.

The crested dwarf iris grows in sandy and rocky woods,
usually in sterile, acidic soil. The pictured specimen was
photographed at Mile 197.8.

Plate 174
Larger Blue Flag Iris *Iris versicolor*

Color: Blue

Bloom: May–August

This beautiful and graceful iris has violet-blue flowers
with prominently veined, yellow-based sepals. The flowers
are supported by sturdy stalks rising amid sword-like
leaves. This plant grows to a height of 2 or 3 feet and is
not unlike the iris that grows in many gardens.

Larger blue flag iris is typically a northern species that
extends southward into North Carolina; thus it is found
mainly in a few locations along the northern section of
the Parkway. Look for it in marshes or wet meadows and

along ditches. The pictured specimen was photographed at the edge of Rakes Mill Pond at Mile 162.4.

Asiatic Dayflower *Commelina communis*
Plate 175

Color: Blue

Bloom: May–October

The reclining stems of this plant have upright, leafy branches with deep blue flowers that protrude from a heart-shaped enfolding leaf. The ½-inch flowers have two rounded blue petals above and a smaller white petal beneath. Three green sepals and six stamens are evident. The leaves are fleshy, oblong to lanceolate, and 3 to 5 inches long, with rounded bases sheathing the stem.

The genus name *Commelina* is based on a Dutch family name, Commelin. Two of the Commelin brothers were renowned botanists, while a third brother died young and unknown; the dayflower's two large blue petals and one small white petal represent the three brothers. The common name for this plant comes from the fact that the blossoms last but a single day.

Dayflower roots, boiled and served with a white sauce, make a tasty substitute for creamed potatoes. Also, the young leaves can be eaten in salads.

This plant is widely distributed and is often found in moist areas and along roadsides. The pictured specimen was photographed at the Bull Creek Valley View parking area at Mile 373.9.

Southern Harebell *Campanula divaricata*
Plate 176

Color: Blue

Bloom: July–October

The southern harebell is the most common of several species of harebell found in the Blue Ridge Mountains. It is a smooth plant with a slender and many-branched stem. Its leaves are lance-shaped to narrowly egg-shaped, pointed at both ends, coarsely and sharply toothed, and up to 3 inches long. From a distance, however, you see only the wiry stems with the nodding blue flowers. Protruding from the center of each flower is a bluish pistil with a tip that is white to pale yellow. The flowers are usually very numerous and arranged in a large but loose cluster.

There are a number of different names for this plant, including bluebell, heatherbell, Lady's Thimble, and Witch's-Bells. It is not clear if the accepted common name "harebell" is for the hares that romp in it or whether perhaps it should be hair-bell for the hair-like stems, or hea'erbell, a contraction of heather-bell. In any case, there is no doubt that the blossoms look like miniature bells.

Southern harebell grows on dry rocky slopes and in open woods. The pictured specimen was photographed at the Thunder Hill Overlook at Mile 208.5.

Plate 177

Closed Gentian *Gentiana clausa*

Color: Blue

Bloom: September–October

The dark blue, bottle-like, nearly closed flowers of this plant are arranged in a tight cluster that rests on a whorl of leaves atop a 1- to 2-foot stem. The 1- to 1½-inch flowers are deep blue, and close inspection will reveal whitish pleats between the five corolla lobes. The ovate leaves form a whorl below the flower cluster, but the lower leaves are in pairs. A similar mountain species, the stiff gentian (*G. quinquefolia*), has clusters of small tubular flowers that open at the top into five bristle-pointed lobes.

Both the closed and the stiff gentian are found on wooded slopes, along streams, and on roadsides. The pictured specimen was photographed at Waterrock Knob at Mile 451.2.

Fringed Phacelia *Phacelia fimbriata*   Plate 178

Color: Blue–White

Bloom: April–May

Fringed phacelia is a pretty little flower that grows in rather large colonies. It is quite uncommon along the Parkway, however, appearing in only a few western North Carolina counties. It is a branching plant with one-sided clusters of light-blue-to-creamy-white flowers. The ½-inch-wide, cup-like blossoms have petals that are uniquely "fringed" along the margins, giving the flower a "lacy" appearance. The 2-inch-long leaves are pinnately divided into five to eleven triangular or oblong lobes. Lower leaves are stalked, upper leaves unstalked.

Though unusual along the Parkway, fringed phacelia is abundant in the Great Smoky Mountains. It grows along streams and in low alluvial woods. The pictured specimen was photographed in a low-lying parking area near the entrance to Linville Falls at Mile 316.5.

Small-flowered Phacelia *Phacelia dubia*   Plate 179

Color: Blue

Bloom: April–May

The small-flowered phacelia is an erect, 5- to 12-inch-tall plant which may or may not be branched at the base. The small, pale blue, five-petaled flowers form a loose cluster atop the stem. The stems are alternately lined with small leaves that may have three or five lobes.

The phacelias belong to the waterleaf family and are sometimes called scorpion-weeds because the leafy stems, topped with a flower cluster, often assume a flat, elongated, arching profile somewhat in the shape of a scorpion's tail. This species grows in woodlands, flood plains, and fields, and along roadsides. The pictured specimen was photographed at the Lane Pinnacle View at Mile 372.

Plate 180

Beard-tongue *Penstemon spp.*

Color: Blue

Bloom: May–July

Atop a stem covered with fine gray down is a loose cluster of showy, tubular, bluish-to-violet flowers. Each 1- to
1½-inch-long flower is two-lipped, with the lower, three-
lobed lip projecting straight out and the upper, two-lobed
lip projecting upward. The lower lip and the "mouth" of
the flower are streaked with dark purple lines. The basal,
ovate leaves are stalked and form a rosette around the
stem. The ovate-to-lanceolate upper leaves clasp the stem.
The gray beard-tongue (*P. canescens*) has smooth midstem
leaves and floral bracts that are much smaller than the
upper leaves. The Small's beard-tongue (*P. smallii*), on the
other hand, has midstem leaves covered with soft hairs
and larger, leaf-like floral bracts.

Beard-tongues are named for the tuft of hairs found on
the sterile stamens. This mountain wildflower was valued
by Indian healers as a remedy for venereal diseases. It
grows on shady banks and along roadsides. The pictured
gray beard-tongue was photographed at the Roanoke
Mountain Overlook on the Roanoke Mountain Loop
Drive at Mile 120.3.

Plate 181

Wild Blue Phlox *Phlox carolina*

Color: Blue

Bloom: May–July

The wild blue phlox has small, five-petaled, trumpet-like
flowers clustered at the top of the stem. The flowers are
normally blue but can range in color from pink to deep
purple. The stem, which is covered with fine hairs, grows
to a height of 3 feet and supports from five to twelve pairs
of lance-shaped, 2- to 4-inch leaves.

The generic name *Phlox* is a Greek term meaning
"flame" and somewhat describes the color of the flower.
Phlox leaves were and still are often crushed and brewed
with water as a potion for curing ailments such as upset
stomach, sore eyes, and skin diseases. An extract made

from the leaves is also used as a laxative. Probably the greatest single virtue of the phlox is its sweet aroma, which is especially strong in the early evening. It often can be detected long before it comes into view.

Wild blue phlox can be found growing in open woods and clearings and along roadsides. The pictured specimen was photographed along the side of the Parkway at Mile 220.

Gill-over-the-ground *Glecoma hederacea* Plate 182

Color: Blue

Bloom: March–June

The small, blue-violet, two-lipped flowers of this ground-hugging plant, also known as ground ivy, are whorled in the axils of dark green, scalloped leaves. The leaves are roundish and have wavy margins. The flower's lower lip is three-lobed, and the fast-growing, creeping stems form large patches in moist shaded or sunny areas.

Gill-over-the-ground is the Americanized version of the French term *guiller*, meaning "to ferment." Both in France and in England the plant was used in the brewing of ale. In 1668, one brewer, Sir Kenelm Digby, reported, "A good handful of ground-ivy leaves, boil'd in a draught of ale, drunk morning and evening; is admirable cure for all head-aches, pains and inflammations."

The pictured specimen was photographed at Mabry Mill at Mile 176.2.

ELONGATED CLUSTERS

Lyre-leaved Sage *Salvia lyrata* Plate 183

Color: Blue

Bloom: April–May

This species is identified by a square, hairy stem that rises from the center of a rosette of 8-inch-long leaves that are deeply lobed into rounded segments. The lavender-blue, tubular, two-lipped flowers surround the stem in whorls of three to ten. The floral whorls occur in several interrupted, spike-like clusters near the top of the stem.

The strange name "lyre-leaved" came about because the leaves supposedly resemble an ancient Greek harp-like musical instrument called a lyre. In some localities it is also known as cancer-weed, but there is no evidence of its ever having caused or having been used to cure cancer. At one time, the fresh leaves were applied to remove warts, and the leaves and seed were made into an ointment to cure wounds and sores.

This plant can be found in open meadows, in woodlands, and along roadsides. The pictured specimen was photographed at the Bull Creek Valley View at Mile 373.9.

Plate 184 **Tufted Vetch** *Vicia cracca*

Color: Blue–Pink

Bloom: May–July

Tufted vetch, also known as cow vetch, is widely scattered along the Parkway and is more likely to be found along the northern section in Virginia. It is a climbing plant with gray-green leaves and a long, one-sided, crowded spike of tubular, blue to pink, pea-like flowers. The flowers hang downward on a long stalk. The leaves are pinnately compound, with eight to ten pairs of narrow, bristly tipped, 1-inch-long leaflets. Look for a pair of tendrils at the end of each stalk.

Spring vetch (*V. sativa*) is somewhat similar to tufted vetch but has rose-pink or purple flowers borne singly or in pairs in the leaf axils. The leaves, tipped with a branched tendril, have eight to sixteen narrow, broad-tipped leaflets.

Both of these species are usually found in waste places, in old fields, and along roadsides. The pictured specimen of tufted vetch was photographed at the Stewart Knob Overlook at Mile 110.9.

Heal-all *Prunella vulgaris*   Plate 185

Color: Blue

Bloom: May–September

This stumpy-looking, low-growing plant is common
in open areas almost everywhere along the Parkway. The
small, bluish lavender flowers grow on cylindrical heads
close to the stalk. The lance-shaped leaves measure up to
4 inches long and often have some shallow teeth along the
margins. As with other members of the mint family, the
leaves are opposite and the stems are square.

Both the common and the botanical names for this
plant refer to the ancient belief in its healing powers.
Because each of the tiny flowers in the cluster appears to
have a mouth and throat, it was once thought the plant
would cure diseases of the mouth and throat. The generic
name *Prunella* was originally *Brunella*, from the German
word meaning "an inflammation of the throat." Heal-all is
also known as Selfheal and is an effective astringent, useful
in stopping the flow of blood from a cut or wound. Also,
it has often been used as a mouthwash by boiling the early
spring leaves in water.

This plant is widely distributed in almost all parts of
the United States and grows on roadsides and in fields,
pastures, and lawns. The pictured specimen was photographed at the Alligator Back Overlook at Mile 243.

Indigo-bush *Amorpha fruticosa*   Plate 186

Color: Blue–Purple

Bloom: June–August

This shrubby member of the pea family is unique in that
its numerous blossoms each consist of a single, bright purple petal wrapped around ten orange, protruding stamens
and are arranged in erect, elongated clusters. The 4- to
12-inch-long compound leaves consist of three to twenty-
five oval, dull green leaflets that are marked with dark
resinous dots. The leaflets are paired along the leafstalk
with the addition of a single terminal leaflet.

The genus name for this plant, *Amorpha*, is from the

Greek word *amorphos*, meaning "deformed," referring to the fact that indigos of this genus have one-petaled flowers as opposed to the four-petaled flowers of indigos of the genus *Baptisia*. Indians made limited use of this plant, making a hot drink similar to tea from the leaves and occasionally crushing the dried leaves for use as a smoking material.

Indigo-bush grows in open, damp woodlands and along streams and rivers. Along the Parkway it is pretty well restricted to the region from Craggy Gardens at Mile 364.5 southward to Raven Fork View at Mile 467.8. The pictured specimen was photographed at Haw Creek Valley Overlook at Mile 380.

Plate 187 **Hyssop Skullcap** *Scutellaria integrifolia*

Color: Blue

Bloom: June–July

Skullcaps have distinctive two-lipped (two-petaled) blossoms with a pale blue, roundish upper lip curving over a flared, usually white, lower lip. The blossoms grow from the axils of bract-like upper leaves and form an elongated cluster. The leaves are opposite, the upper ones being lanceolate and untoothed and the lower ones broader and toothed. A similar species, the heart-leaved skullcap (*S. ovata*), can also be found along the Parkway; it is slightly hairy and its leaves have a heart-shaped base.

The word "hyssop" is biblical in origin and is derived from the Hebrew word *ezov*, which refers to a plant used by ancient Hebrews in rites of purification: "Ye shall take a bunch of hyssop and dip" (Exodus 12:22). No doubt this plant resembles the hyssop used by the Hebrews.

Hyssop skullcaps are usually found in low meadows and along woodland borders from Mile 240 north. The pictured specimen was photographed at the edge of the meadow below Stone Mountain Overlook at Mile 232.5.

Tall Bellflower *Campanula americana* Plate 188

Color: Blue–Violet

Bloom: June–September

This plant belongs to the bluebell family, of which there are about 900 widely distributed species. The tall bell-flower, which grows to a height of nearly 6 feet, features light blue flowers that emerge from the upper leaf axils and form a spike-like cluster. Each flower has a flat, five-part corolla which is occasionally tubular. A long, distinctive, curving and recurving filament known as the style protrudes from the corolla's center. The flower rests on a bed of leaf-like bracts. The leaves are long, thin, ovate to lanceolate, and toothed.

Despite the common name "bellflower" and the genus name *Campanula*, which is from the Latin word for "bell," the flowers of this species are often flat rather than bell-shaped.

This is a rather common mountain wildflower that grows in rich deciduous woods and in clearings. The pictured specimen was photographed at the Waynesville View at Mile 440.8.

Great Lobelia *Lobelia siphilitica* Plate 189

Color: Blue

Bloom: August–October

This tall, showy plant features bright blue flowers that rise from leafy bracts and form an elongated cluster. The lower lip of the two-lipped flower is striped with white and is tipped by five pointed lobes. The 2- to 6-inch-long leaves are ovate to lanceolate and may be toothed or untoothed.

According to Benjamin Franklin's 1751 reprint of *Medicina Britannica*, a concoction made from the roots of this plant was discovered by Indians to be effective in curing venereal disease, hence the plant's species name. This supposed "cure" for syphilis spread to England and Europe before studies eventually showed that it was useless.

Great lobelia is chiefly a mountain species and can be

found in wet meadows, in low woods, and along stream banks. The pictured specimen was photographed at the Lickstone Ridge Overlook at Mile 458.9.

VINES AND SHRUBS

Plate 190

Butterfly Pea *Clitoria mariana*

Color: Blue

Bloom: June–August

This low, smooth, twining vine sports large, pale blue, pea-like flowers of unusual beauty. Its compound leaves are divided into three ovate, toothless leaflets, and it gains support from inanimate objects through the use of long, winding tendrils. The plant's small pea-like seeds are encased in a 2-inch-long, flattened pod, which splits into two twisted halves at maturity.

At one time it was believed that the butterfly pea might have medicinal value as a treatment for infertility, but no scientific evidence supports that belief. The plant is found in open woods, in clearings, and along roadsides. The pictured specimen was photographed at the Otter Lake Parking Area at Mile 63.

ALL SHAPES

Flame Azalea *Rhododendron calendulaceum* Plate 191

Color: Orange

Bloom: May–July

This beautiful mountain shrub is one of the earliest blooming azaleas and is the only one with orange blossoms. The clusters of tubular, vase-shaped flowers range in color from bright orange to red to yellow. The deciduous, ovate leaves are 2 to 4 inches long.

This handsome plant presents striking displays along the forest edges and on grassy balds. The pictured specimen was photographed near the parking area at the Fox Hunter's Paradise Overlook at Mile 218.7.

Butterfly-weed *Asclepias tuberosa* Plate 192

Color: Orange

Bloom: May–August

Butterfly-weed's clusters of bright orange flowers crown a leafy, hairy stem. The clusters are magnificent, and where they merge in large patches, they form beautiful, bright orange blankets. Each flower in the cluster is about ⅜ inch across and has five orange-colored, curved-back petals. The leaves are alternate, oblong to narrow, and smooth.

As its name implies, this brilliant flower attracts many butterflies, as well as a host of honeybees. Throughout its range it is known by many different names, including pleurisy-root, chigger flower, orange milkweed, silkweed, and others.

Indians boiled the roots in water and drank the decoction to treat pleurisy. In some areas, this plant is still known as pleurisy-root. Also, the fresh roots were ground into a powder and used as a poultice for open wounds.

Butterfly-weed can be seen growing in open fields and on open rocky slopes throughout the summer. The pic-

ALL SHAPES

Plate 196

Red Trillium *Trillium erectum*

Color: Red

Bloom: March–June

In the trilliums, all parts are in threes. This plant, known also as Wake Robin, has a nodding, three-petaled flower rising on a stalk above a whorl of three broadly ovate, diamond-shaped leaves. The flower, with petals that might range in color from deep purple to maroon to pink, includes also a greenish central disk and three green sepals "peeking" out from between the petals.

This is a foul-smelling plant that attracts carrion flies to act as pollinators. This explains one of its other common names, Stinking-Benjamin. In some areas of New England, perhaps because of the strong odor, its popular name is Nose Bleed.

This common member of the lily family is usually found in moist wooded areas. The pictured specimen was photographed at Mabry Mill at Mile 176.2.

Plate 197

Indian Paint Brush *Castilleja coccinea*

Color: Red

Bloom: April–June

Actually, the flowers of this unusual member of the snapdragon family are hidden within the axils of the scarlet-tipped, fan-shaped bracts arranged in a dense spike at the top of the stem. The basal leaves are 1 to 3 inches long, elliptic, untoothed, and arranged in a rosette. The stalkless stem leaves are divided into narrow segments.

Many of the various Indian tribes throughout North America collected and used this plant for medicinal purposes. A solution made from the roots, taken in small amounts as a drink, is said to have been a cure for venereal diseases. Indian paint brush grows in meadows and fields and in damp sandy soil. The pictured specimen was photographed at Linville Caverns on Route 221 (exit the Parkway at Mile 317.5).

Columbine *Aquilegia canadensis*

Plate 198

Color: Red

Bloom: April–May

Columbines, with their drooping, bell-shaped, red flowers, are unmistakable. The flower's five long and curved spurs, along with the stamen that protrudes from the center of the five petals in the form of a long yellow column, are unique features. Further, the leaves are divided and subdivided into threes.

The name "columbine" is from the Latin word *columba*, meaning "dove." Supposedly, the shape and proportions of the leaflets resemble the tail of a dove. Also known as red bells, this plant, with its persistent fragrance, was widely used by Indian tribes as a perfume. The fragrance was obtained by crushing and chewing the lustrous, black seeds into a paste which was then spread among clothing, where the sweet odor persisted for a long time.

Columbines grow in rich, rocky woods, in pastures, and along roadsides. The pictured specimen was photographed at Mile 183.7.

Common Lousewort *Pedicularis canadensis*

Plate 199

Color: Red–Yellow

Bloom: April–May

This rather hairy plant, known variously as common lousewort or wood betony, has flowers that might be red, yellow, or red and yellow forming a short but dense terminal cluster. Each flower is about ¾ inch long, with petals uniting to form an upper and lower lip. The upper, arched lip appears to have two small teeth; the shorter lower lip is three-lobed and spreading. Leaf-like bracts support the flower. The hairy leaves are up to 5 inches long, oblong, and deeply divided into toothed lobes.

The plant is known as common lousewort because it

was once believed that cattle grazing on or among the plants became covered with lice. Early settlers brewed a tea from the leaves to settle upset stomachs and, thinking the plant to be a strong herb, they called it wood betony. Betony is from the Latin word *betonica*, which is a variation of *vettonica*, meaning "herb." Some Indian tribes used the leaves as a poultice to reduce external swelling.

This plant is found mainly in the mountains in open woodlands and forest edges. The pictured specimen was photographed near the Moses Cone Manor and Craft Shop at Mile 294.

Plate 200 **Leather-flower** *Clematis viorna*

Color: Red–Purple

Bloom: July–October

This is a climbing vine that finds support on other low-growing bushes and shrubs. Of special interest is the unusual flower, which is solitary, nodding, bell-shaped, and purplish to dull red, and has sepals (petals are absent) that feel leathery to the touch. Despite its leathery texture, the flower does have a rather sweet scent. As the flowers mature, they give way to plume-like clumps of fruit. The leaves are opposite and divided into three to seven ovate and bright green leaflets.

Because the nodding flower looks much like a miniature vase, this plant is also known in some areas as the Vase-vine. Another name, Old-Man's Whiskers, results from the plume-like clumps of fruit.

This plant can be found in rich open woods, in clear-ings, and along roadsides. The pictured specimen was pho-tographed at the Mahogany Rock Overlook at Mile 235.

Plate 201 **Bee-balm** *Monarda didyma*

Color: Red

Bloom: July–September

This plant's rounded cluster of bright red flowers is perched atop a sturdy, square stem. Each flower is about 1½ inches long and consists of two lips, five lobes, and two projecting stamens. The floral cluster rests on a "bed" of reddish bracts. The leaves are 3 to 6 inches long, dark green, ovate, and coarsely toothed.

Bee-balm is also known as Oswego Tea, because it was the Oswego Indians of New York who first discovered that a refreshing and healthful drink could be made from the leaves. This plant does attract a lot of bees, and the spicy aromatic odor might have a soothing affect on them, so perhaps that is why it is called bee-balm.

It grows to a height of 5 feet and is usually found in damp areas and along wooded streams. The pictured specimen was photographed in the River Bend Parking Area near the Linville Falls Recreation Area at Mile 316.5.

ALL SHAPES

Plate 202
Jack-in-the-Pulpit *Arisaema triphyllum*

Color: Green

Bloom: April–May

This plant features a greenish, vase-like flower (the pulpit) with a flap-like hood curving over the top. The pulpit contains an erect, club-like spadix (Jack) which bears tiny separate male and female blooms near the base. "Jack," in his canopied "pulpit," is perched beneath the shade of one or two large leaves. The leaves are three-parted, veined, and dull green. By late summer, a cluster of shiny red berries forms on the spadix.

This plant is known by many names, including Indian-turnip, Bog-Onion, and Poison-in-the-Pulpit. It has been reported that the spadix, when fresh, contains a severely acrid juice that imparts a caustic sensation to mucous membranes when chewed. Schoolboys tricked into taking a bite of the spadix give rise to another common name, Memory-root, as the effects are never forgotten.

Jack-in-the-Pulpit grows in rich moist woods and bogs. The pictured specimen was photographed near the Moses Cone Mansion and Craft Shop at Mile 294.

Plate 203
Solomon's Seal *Polygonatum biflorum*

Color: Green

Bloom: April–June

This is a low-growing plant common to rocky woods, thickets, and forest edges. The arching stem is 1 to 3 feet long with a number of evenly spaced, alternate, ovate, and untoothed leaves. The ½-inch-long, greenish white flowers hang like tiny bells from the leaf axils. By early August, the blossoms are transformed into round, bluish black berries.

The generic name *Polygonatum* is derived from the Greek

words *poly* and *gonum*, meaning "many jointed" and referring to the number of joints in the rootstock. The species
name *biflorum* refers to the flowers, which hang in pairs.
The most widely accepted origin for the common name
comes from the fact that the rootstock has scars that are
shaped somewhat like a signet used as a royal seal. The
plant's namesake, of course, is King Solomon, the tenth-
century B.C. king of Israel who was famed for his wisdom
and who, it was thought, possessed great knowledge concerning medicinal herbs. It was believed that he placed his
seal of approval on this plant, that is, the Solomon's seal.

Indians and early mountain settlers boiled and ate the
starchy roots like potatoes and also ground the dried roots
into flour. The leaves were crushed and used as a poultice
to soothe scrapes and bruises.

The pictured specimen was photographed at the
entrance to the old cable-car road at Mile 234.

Bluebead-lily *Clintonia borealis*

Plate 204

Color: Green–Yellow

Bloom: May–June

This plant has a 6- to 12-inch-tall stem rising from a
basal set of two or three bright green, oblong leaves. Atop
the leafless stem nod three to six greenish yellow, bell-like
flowers. Each flower consists of three petals and three
petal-like sepals. Six stamens protrude from the flower's
center. The 5- to 8-inch-long basal leaves are upright and
smooth.

This lovely flower, which is often found in large colonies, is known as bluebead-lily because of the shiny, oval,
pure blue but tasteless berries that appear at summer's
end. Other names include corn-lily and yellow clintonia.

Folks in the "high-country" of Maine call this plant
Cow-tongue and use the very young leaves extensively as
a potherb. The clintonias were named in honor of New
York governor DeWitt Clinton (1769–1828). Governor
Clinton began his political career when he was elected
mayor of New York City in 1803 and later went on to
become a state senator, lieutenant governor, and presiden-

75 Best Sites

❀ Indicates "blue ribbon" sites, not to be missed by
  wildflower enthusiasts.

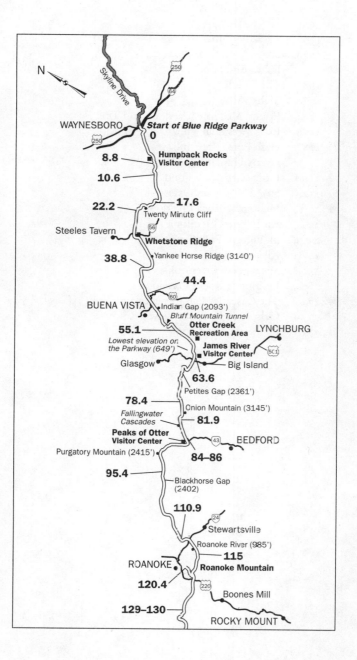

N

Skyline Drive

250

64

WAYNESBORO

250

Start of Blue Ridge Parkway
0

8.8 — **Humpback Rocks**
Visitor Center

10.6

22.2 — **17.6**

Twenty Minute Cliff

56

Steeles Tavern

Whetstone Ridge

• Yankee Horse Ridge (3140')

38.8

44.4

60

BUENA VISTA

• Indian Gap (2093')
Bluff Mountain Tunnel

Otter Creek
Recreation Area

55.1

Lowest elevation on
the Parkway (649')

Glasgow

James River
Visitor Center

Big Island

LYNCHBURG

5C1

63.6

Petites Gap (2361')

78.4 — • Onion Mountain (3145')

Fallingwater
Cascades

81.9

Peaks of Otter
Visitor Center

43

BEDFORD

Purgatory Mountain (2415')•

84–86

95.4 —

Blackhorse Gap
(2402)

110.9

24

• Stewartsville

• Roanoke River (985')

115

ROANOKE

Roanoke Mountain

120.4

220

Boones Mill

129–130 —

ROCKY MOUNT

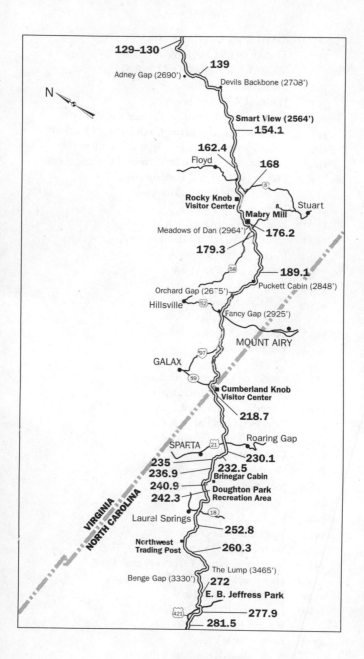

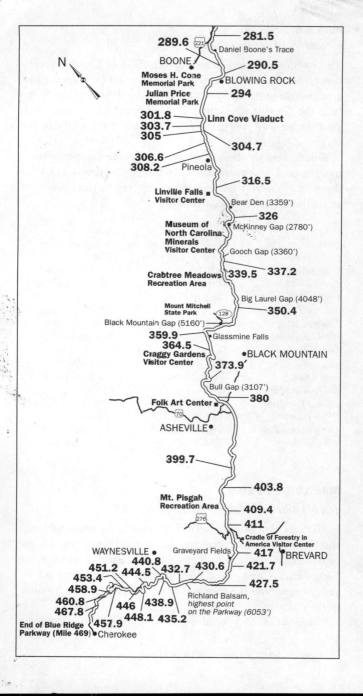

N

281.5
289.6
221
Daniel Boone's Trace
BOONE
290.5
Moses H. Cone
Memorial Park
BLOWING ROCK
Julian Price
Memorial Park
294
301.8
Linn Cove Viaduct
303.7
305
304.7
306.6
308.2
Pineola
316.5
Linville Falls
Visitor Center
Bear Den (3359')
326
Museum of
North Carolina
Minerals
Visitor Center
McKinney Gap (2780')
Gooch Gap (3360')
Crabtree Meadows
339.5
337.2
Recreation Area
Big Laurel Gap (4048')
Mount Mitchell
State Park
128
350.4
Black Mountain Gap (5160')
Glassmine Falls
359.9
364.5
BLACK MOUNTAIN
Craggy Gardens
Visitor Center
373.9'
Bull Gap (3107')
Folk Art Center
380
70
ASHEVILLE
399.7
403.8
Mt. Pisgah
Recreation Area
409.4
276
411
Cradle of Forestry in
America Visitor Center
WAYNESVILLE
Graveyard Fields
417
BREVARD
440.8
432.7
430.6
421.7
451.2
444.5
453.4
427.5
458.9
460.8
446
438.9
Richland Balsam,
467.8
448.1
435.2
highest point
on the Parkway (6053')
End of Blue Ridge
457.9
Parkway (Mile 469)
Cherokee

Mile 8.8

Greenstone Parking Area

This overlook is perched atop a formation of Catoctin greenstone, rock formed by ancient lava flows that inundated a vast area stretching from what is now Maryland to Virginia. Nearby is the Greenstone Nature Trail, a leisurely, 20-minute, self-guided tour with trail markers that explain the geology of the surrounding mountains.

Wildflowers are abundant here, and include the special summer treats of wild stonecrop and whorled rosinweed. Look for the wild stonecrop growing from crevices in the rocky cliff along the entrance to the overlook.

SPRING
Field Pansy
Common Blue Violet
Wild Strawberry
Garlic Mustard
Pinxter-flower
Meadow Parsnip
Common Winter Cress
Wild Geranium
Smooth Rock-cress

SUMMER
Yellow Wood Sorrel
Bladder Campion
White Campion
Queen Anne's Lace
Wild Stonecrop

Solomon's Seal
Yellow Goat's-beard
Purple-flowering
    Raspberry
Yellow Sweet Clover
Deptford Pink
Daisy Fleabane
White Sweet Clover
Gray Beard-tongue
Goldenrods
Heal-all
Woolly Mullein
Southern Harebell
Evening Primrose
Wild Mint
Narrow-leaved
    Houstonia

Bouncing Bet
Poke Milkweed
Asiatic Dayflower
Pale Touch-me-not
Whorled Rosinweed

FALL
Yellow Wood Sorrel
Bouncing Bet
Poke Milkweed
Asiatic Dayflower
Pale Touch-me-not
Goldenrods
White-flowered Asters
Blue-flowered Asters
Butter-and-eggs
White Snakeroot

Mile 10.6 and 10.9

Rock Point and Raven's Roost Overlooks

Both these overlooks have similar views to the northeast, over the Great Valley as it stretches out to the far horizon. To the northwest, a few miles distant, is the eastern end of Torry Ridge. Back Creek, paralleled by Route 64, runs through the valley below, and the community of Sherando Camp is visible in the distance.

Wildflowers of special interest here include springtime

round-leaved yellow violets, summer sundrops, and fall butter-and-eggs.

SPRING
Shepherd's-purse
Common Blue Violet
Garlic Mustard
Common Winter Cress
Wild Geranium
Early Saxifrage
Round-leaved Yellow
  Violet
Golden Alexander
Solomon's Seal

SUMMER
White Campion
Solomon's Seal
Bowman's-root

Bladder Campion
Sundrops
Yellow Sweet Clover
Daisy Fleabane
Yarrow
Spotted Knapweed
Greater Coreopsis
Common Milkweed
Goldenrods
Woodland Sunflower
Green-headed
  Coneflower
Narrow-leaved
  Houstonia
Yellow Wood Sorrel
Starry Campion

Southern Harebell
Queen Anne's Lace

FALL
Yellow Wood Sorrel
White Campion
Queen Anne's Lace
Woodland Sunflower
Green-headed
  Coneflower
White-flowered Asters
Goldenrods
Blue-flowered Asters
Butter-and-eggs
Spotted Knapweed
White Snakeroot

Mile 17.6

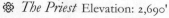 *The Priest* Elevation: 2,690'

Priest Mountain (elevation 4,056'), for which this overlook is named, is visible 5 miles directly to the south. It is the highest of the "Religious Mountains," a group that also includes Little Priest, Cardinal, and Bald Friar. Also visible is Maintop Mountain (elevation 4,039'), 6 miles to the southwest, and Three-Ridges Mountain (elevation 3,900'), 4 miles to the southeast. Several large hickory trees grow here, and they are described by a nearby Park Service exhibit.

A grassy path leading to the nearby Torry Ridge View passes through a jungle of late summer and early fall wildflowers. During this time, milkweed blossoms attract large numbers of butterflies. Often as many as eight or ten can be seen crowded on a single cluster of blossoms.

SPRING
Shepherd's-purse
Kidneyleaf Buttercup
Wild Strawberry

Common Blue Violet
Common Winter Cress
Giant Chickweed
Garlic Mustard

Dwarf Cinquefoil
Flowering Dogwood
Cleavers
Cut-leaf Toothwort

SUMMER	Queen Anne's Lace	FALL
Golden Ragwort	Heal-all	Common Milkweed
Mouse-ear Hawkweed	Goldenrods	Queen Anne's Lace
Bladder Campion	New York Ironweed	Hoary Tick-trefoil
Hop Clover	Sweet Joe-pye-weed	Virgin's Bower
Daisy Fleabane	Field Thistle	White-flowered Asters
Yellow Goat's-beard	Common Milkweed	Field Thistle
Yarrow	Hoary Tick-trefoil	Heal-all
Deptford Pink	Virgin's Bower	New York Ironweed
Hairy Hawkweed	White-flowered Asters	Wild Bean
Thimbleweed		Goldenrods
Ox-eye Daisy		White Snakeroot

Mile 22.2

Bald Mountain Overlook Elevation: 3,252'

Bald Mountain rears up just to the left of this overlook. The mountain was named nearly 200 years ago when its "baldness" was more evident. The "bald" was created by the constant movement of rock rubble along the slopes. Today the forests have moved in and stabilized the slopes, allowing the growth of an understory of ground cover. As a result, Bald Mountain is no longer bald.

Nearby the overlook is the entrance to an easy-to-walk, U.S. Forest Service trail that runs for about a mile to the site of an old fire tower. Many wildflowers can be found along the trail as well as around the overlook.

SPRING	Bowman's-root	Flowering Spurge
Common Blue Violet	Golden Alexander	Goldenrods
Wild Strawberry	Common Lousewort	
Flowering Dogwood	Yellow Wood Sorrel	FALL
Common Winter Cress	Hop Clover	Queen Anne's Lace
Garlic Mustard	Yarrow	Yellow Wood Sorrel
Dwarf Cinquefoil	Yellow Sweet Clover	Flowering Spurge
Wild Geranium	Gray Beard-tongue	Woodland Sunflower
	Sundrops	Goldenrods
SUMMER	Evening Primrose	White Snakeroot
Mouse-ear Hawkweed	Queen Anne's Lace	Blue-flowered Asters
King Devil	White Avens	

Mile 38.8

Boston Knob Overlook Elevation: 2,523'

This small overlook is perched on the edge of Boston Mountain and has a view to the northeast over Irish Creek Valley. Irish Creek courses along the valley for about 5 miles before emptying into the South River. Visible across the valley are Adam's Peak and McClung Mountain.

The small field between the parking area and the Parkway is a mecca of wildflowers, including specialties such as sweet cicely in the spring, yellow goat's-beard in the summer, and closed gentian in the fall.

SPRING
Henbit
Gill-over-the-ground
Field Pansy
Wild Strawberry
Flowering Dogwood
Common Winter Cress
Blackberry
Common Buttercup
Wild Geranium
Dwarf Cinquefoil
Yellow Wood Sorrel
Plantain-leaved
   Pussytoes
Sweet Cicely

SUMMER
Golden Ragwort
King Devil
Yellow Wood Sorrel
Yellow Goat's-beard
Yarrow
Queen Anne's Lace
Daisy Fleabane
Ox-eye Daisy
Black-eyed Susan
Solomon's Seal
Flowering Spurge
Hop Clover
Deptford Pink
Thimbleweed
Wild Bergamot
Rough Avens
Heal-all

Common Milkweed
Spotted Knapweed
Field Thistle
Asiatic Dayflower
Pigeonberry
White-flowered Asters

FALL
Queen Anne's Lace
Horse-nettle
Yellow Wood Sorrel
White-flowered Asters
Blue-flowered Asters
Hoary Tick-trefoil
Field Thistle
Goldenrods
White Snakeroot
Closed Gentian

Mile 44.4

White's Gap Overlook Elevation: 2,567'

White's Gap, directly below this overlook, separates White's Peak from Bald Knob, which is visible in the distance to the southeast. At one time the gap was the main "over-the-ridge" crossing point for the old Jordan toll road. The Pedlar River courses along the floor of the gap, and a section of the Appalachian Trail follows the crest of Bald Knob.

A variety of wildflowers can be found here, beginning with

henbit in the spring and ending with woodland sunflowers in the fall.

SPRING	SUMMER	
Henbit	Mouse-ear Hawkweed	Sweet Joe-pye-weed
Bird's-eye Speedwell	Rough-fruited	Woodland Sunflower
Common Blue Violet	Cinquefoil	Heal-all
Wild Strawberry	White Campion	Hoary Tick-trefoil
Giant Chickweed	Flowering Spurge	Southern Harebell
Common Winter Cress	Common Milkweed	White-flowered Asters
Flowering Dogwood	Hop Clover	
Pinxter-flower	Yellow Wood Sorrel	FALL
Wild Geranium	Japanese Honeysuckle	Flowering Spurge
Garlic Mustard	Solomon's Seal	Horse-nettle
Blackberry	Yarrow	White Campion
Cleavers	New Jersey Tea	Yellow Wood Sorrel
Golden Alexander	Deptford Pink	Heal-all
Dovesfoot Cranesbill	Gray Beard-tongue	Hoary Tick-trefoil
Perfoliate Bellwort	Greater Coreopsis	Goldenrods
Solomon's Seal	Thimbleweed	White-flowered Asters
		Woodland Sunflower

Mile 55.1

White Oak Flats Overlook Elevation: 1,460'

As the name implies, the flats below this overlook are covered with a stand of massive white oak trees, some of which are more than a century old. The oaks thrive well along the moist and nourishing banks of Dancing Creek, which runs through the valley below.

This is an especially good spot for close-up views of the colorful fall foliage, which is intensified by the bright colors of fall asters and goldenrods.

SPRING	Yellow Wood Sorrel	Yellow Star-grass
Bluets	Mouse-ear Chickweed	Yarrow
Wild Strawberry	Rattlesnake-weed	Deptford Pink
Dwarf Cinquefoil		Spotted Wintergreen
Giant Chickweed	SUMMER	Whorled Coreopsis
Flowering Dogwood	Mouse-ear Hawkweed	Daisy Fleabane
Common Cinquefoil	Golden Ragwort	Queen Anne's Lace
Yellow Star-grass	Hop Clover	Spotted Knapweed

Ox-eye Daisy	FALL	Heal-all
Greater Coreopsis	Queen Anne's Lace	Goldenrods
Heal-all	Yarrow	Silverrod
Goldenrods	Lance-leaved Coreopsis	Blue-flowered Asters
	Spotted Knapweed	White-flowered Asters

Mile 63.6

❀ *James River Visitor Center and Museum* Elevation: 647'

A stop at the James River Visitor Center and Museum is time well spent. The museum is educational as well as entertaining, and a visit to the restored lock and canal on the river is a walk back into history. Otter Creek flows past the parking area here and rushes on for a short distance to empty into the James River.

Spring wildflowers are abundant here, especially along the nearby Trail of Trees. Special springtime treats along the trail include wild blue phlox, early saxifrage, and wild stonecrop.

SPRING	Plantain-leaved	White Avens
Bloodroot	Pussytoes	Yellow Wood Sorrel
Bluets	Yellow Wood Sorrel	Narrow-leaved
Purple Dead Nettle	Golden Ragwort	Houstonia
Bird's-eye Speedwell	Wild Blue Phlox	Spotted Touch-me-not
Gill-over-the-ground	Spiderwort	English Plantain
Kidneyleaf Buttercup	False Solomon's-seal	Woolly Mullein
Flowering Dogwood	Common Fleabane	Goldenrods
Common Chickweed	Solomon's Seal	Asiatic Dayflower
Early Saxifrage		White Snakeroot
Dwarf Cinquefoil	SUMMER	
Bulbous Buttercup	Solomon's Seal	FALL
Crested Dwarf Iris	Golden Ragwort	White-flowered Asters
Wild Stonecrop	Wild Stonecrop	Yellow Wood Sorrel
Garlic Mustard	Spotted Wintergreen	White Snakeroot
Cleavers	Daisy Fleabane	Goldenrods
Golden Ragwort	Yarrow	Silverrod

Mile 78.4

Sunset Fields

The parking area at Sunset Fields provides access to the Apple Orchard Falls Trail. The trail intersects the Appalachian Trail about 1,000 feet from the parking area, then continues on 1.5 miles to Apple Orchard Falls on North Creek.

The open fields bordering the overlook are filled with a variety of summer and fall wildflowers. From mid- to late summer, see if you can find the white, trumpet-like flowers of the hedge bindweed along the edge of the overlook.

SPRING
Shepherd's-purse
Common Blue Violet
Wild Strawberry
Common Winter Cress
Giant Chickweed
Dwarf Cinquefoil

SUMMER
Hop Clover
Yarrow
Queen Anne's Lace
Daisy Fleabane
Bladder Campion
Common Milkweed

White Campion
Heal-all
Ox-eye Daisy
Horse-nettle
Common St. John's-wort
Whorled Loosestrife
Evening Primrose
Pale Touch-me-not
Black Cohosh
Wild Bergamot
Pale Indian-plantain
Ox-eye
Yellow Wood Sorrel
Black-eyed Susan

Spotted Knapweed
Hedge Bindweed
White Snakeroot

FALL
Yellow Wood Sorrel
Evening Primrose
Queen Anne's Lace
Pale Touch-me-not
Spotted Knapweed
Hedge Bindweed
Goldenrods
Jimsonweed
White Snakeroot
White-flowered Asters

Mile 81.9

Headforemost Mountain View Elevation: 2,860′

Headforemost Mountain is the tall, cone-shaped peak across the valley to the right. It rises to an elevation of 3,725 feet and slopes down to the base of Flat Top Mountain, the tallest but least known of the Peaks of Otter. A Park Service exhibit here describes one of the Parkway's more common trees, the yellow poplar, also known as the tulip tree. Two excellent specimens can be seen near the entrance to the overlook.

Also found here is common lousewort, a most interesting plant that is semiparasitic, obtaining some of its nourishment from the roots of other plants. Don't be afraid to touch it; the plant is not covered with lice as was believed by early settlers.

SPRING
Purple Dead Nettle
Shepherd's-purse
Common Blue Violet

Common Winter Cress
Giant Chickweed
Flowering Dogwood
Wild Strawberry

Gill-over-the-ground
Dwarf Cinquefoil
Common Cinquefoil
Garlic Mustard

Bulbous Buttercup
Dovesfoot Cranesbill
Common Lousewort
Wild Geranium
Yellow Wood Sorrel
Golden Alexander
King Devil

SUMMER
Hairy Hawkweed
Golden Alexander
Hop Clover
White Campion

Deptford Pink
Ox-eye Daisy
Queen Anne's Lace
Yarrow
Daisy Fleabane
Yellow Goat's-beard
Black-eyed Susan
Pale Touch-me-not
Tall Bellflower
Greater Coreopsis
Sweet Joe-pye-weed
White-flowered Asters
Ox-eye

Woodland Sunflower
Asiatic Dayflower

FALL
Yellow Wood Sorrel
White-flowered Asters
Pale Touch-me-not
Woodland Sunflower
Asiatic Dayflower
Goldenrods
White Snakeroot

Miles 84–86
❀ *Peaks of Otter Lodge and Recreation Area*

The Peaks of Otter Recreation Area includes camping facilities, a spacious and scenic picnic area, a service station and camp store, hiking trails, and the lodge.

The campground is divided into an area for tents and pop-up campers and another for travel trailers and motor homes. Though all campsites are primitive, they are equipped with a picnic table and a fireplace. No hook-ups are available, but fresh water and restrooms are nearby. All these facilities are open from May 1 to November 1, with the exception of the lodge, which consists of a restaurant and motel and is open year-round. The restaurant is open daily from 7:30 A.M. to 8:30 P.M. The motel features spacious rooms with two double beds, private bath, and breathtaking views over Abbott Lake, named for Stanley Abbott (1908–1975), the first resident landscape architect and planner of the Blue Ridge Parkway. From spring through fall, reservations are recommended for the lodge (540-586-1081).

Wildflowers here are many and varied. The best places to look for them are in the picnic area and around the edge of Abbott Lake.

SPRING
Skunk Cabbage
Kidneyleaf Buttercup
Common Blue Violet

Wild Strawberry
Gill-over-the-ground
Purple Dead Nettle
Early Winter Cress

Garlic Mustard
Dwarf Cinquefoil
Yellow Wood Sorrel
Flowering Dogwood

Wild Geranium
Periwinkle
Golden Ragwort
King Devil
Bulbous Buttercup
Spiderwort
Lettuce Saxifrage

SUMMER
King Devil
Spiderwort
Yellow Wood Sorrel

White Campion
Black Cohosh
Water Hemlock
Hedge Bindweed
Yarrow
Ox-eye Daisy
Common Milkweed
Queen Anne's Lace
Rough Avens
English Plantain
Asiatic Dayflower
White Snakeroot

FALL
Yellow Wood Sorrel
White Campion
Heal-all
Crown-beard
Queen Anne's Lace
White Snakeroot
Arrow-leaf Tearthumb
White-flowered Asters
Long-bristled
 Smartweed
Peruvian Daisy

Mile 95.4

Harvey's Knob Elevation: 2,524'

The view at Harvey's Knob is to the northwest, over the Great Valley. This is one of three sites along the Blue Ridge Parkway for observing the annual fall migration of the birds of prey. The other two sites are Rockfish Gap at Mile 0 and Mahogany Rock at Mile 235. Each fall, southward-migrating raptors follow the mountain ridges, and thousands pass this way. Two Park Service exhibits here describe the migration and the migrating raptors. Migration observations begin in early September and end in late November.

While the raptor migration is the main attraction at this overlook, the abundance of wildflowers here is also impressive. The wildflower season begins in March with the appearance of shepherd's-purse and ends with the goldenrods in November.

SPRING
Shepherd's-purse
Henbit
Field Pansy
Wild Strawberry
Purple Dead Nettle
Flowering Dogwood
Blackberry
Tufted Vetch
Common Winter Cress
King Devil
Wild Geranium
Dovesfoot Cranesbill

Bulbous Buttercup
Solomon's Seal

SUMMER
Hop Clover
Dovesfoot Cranesbill
King Devil
English Plantain
Common Buttercup
Rough-fruited
 Cinquefoil
Daisy Fleabane
New Jersey Tea

Yellow Sweet Clover
Ox-eye Daisy
Yarrow
Sundrops
Queen Anne's Lace
Greater Coreopsis
Woolly Mullein
Evening Primrose
Jimsonweed
Asiatic Dayflower
Goldenrods
Field Thistle
Woodland Sunflower

FALL
Asiatic Dayflower
Jimsonweed
Queen Anne's Lace

Spotted Knapweed
Yellow Wood Sorrel
White-flowered Asters
Woodland Sunflower

White Snakeroot
Tall Thistle
Goldenrods

Mile 110.9

Stewart Knob Overlook Elevation: 1,365'

This overlook, a short distance off the Parkway, has an excellent view over the city of Roanoke, Virginia. In the evening, the lights of the city sparkle like a sky full of stars. The city offers many fine attractions, including the Virginia Museum of Transportation, the Science Museum of Western Virginia, the Museum of Fine Arts, and the Mill Mountain Zoological Park and Wildflower Gardens.

From mid- to late May, the embankments around this overlook are blanketed with the bright blue and deep green of tufted vetch intermingled with pink Honesty and yellow goat's-beard.

SPRING
Shepherd's-purse
Bird's-eye Speedwell
Purple Dead Nettle
Yellow Wood Sorrel
Hop Clover
Garlic Mustard
Honesty
Cleavers
Blackberry
Corn Gromwell
Dovesfoot Cranesbill
Common Fleabane
Tufted Vetch
Yellow Goat's-beard

SUMMER
Hop Clover
Yellow Goat's-beard
Tufted Vetch
Honesty
Dovesfoot Cranesbill
Yellow Wood Sorrel
Daisy Fleabane
Japanese Honeysuckle
Rough-fruited
 Cinquefoil
White Campion
Yarrow
Horse-nettle
Spotted Knapweed
Hedge Bindweed
Smooth Hawk's-beard

Pigeonberry
Woolly Mullein
Common Morning
 Glory
Bouncing Bet

FALL
Yellow Wood Sorrel
Hedge Bindweed
Pigeonberry
Common Morning
 Glory
Bouncing Bet
Spotted Knapweed
Crown-beard
Goldenrods

Mile 115

Explore Park

Explore Park offers the opportunity to experience southwest Virginia's rich cultural history and to enjoy its diverse geology, plants, and wildlife. Costumed interpreters explain eighteenth- and nineteenth-century farm and frontier life in a reconstructed settlement. Naturalists and photographers will enjoy the more than 13 miles of hiking trails. A nominal entry fee is charged. The park is open Saturday through Monday from early April to early October.

Of special interest here are the stands of chicory growing along the edges of the entry road and the large crop of purple dead nettle growing near the restored settlement.

SPRING
Shepherd's-purse
Purple Dead Nettle
Early Winter Cress
Henbit
Common Blue Violet
Wild Strawberry
Flowering Dogwood
Blackberry
Common Fleabane
Dwarf Cinquefoil
Sweet White Violet
Yellow Wood Sorrel
May-apple
Common Winter Cress
Hop Clover

SUMMER
Daisy Fleabane
Chicory
White Sweet Clover
Yellow Sweet Clover
Hop Clover
Yellow Wood Sorrel
White Campion
Ox-eye Daisy
Spotted Knapweed
Japanese Honeysuckle
Woolly Mullein
Hedge Bindweed
Common Milkweed
English Plantain
Pigeonberry
Black-eyed Susan

Queen Anne's Lace
Greater Coreopsis
Woodland Sunflower
Goldenrods

FALL
Daisy Fleabane
Woodland Sunflower
Queen Anne's Lace
Yellow Wood Sorrel
Pigeonberry
Upland Boneset
Crown-beard
White Snakeroot
Goldenrods
White-flowered Asters

Mile 120.4

Fishburn Parkway Spur Road, and Mill Mountain Zoological Park and Wildflower Garden

The Fishburn Parkway Spur Road leads to several points of interest that are only a short distance off the Parkway. The Gum Spring Overlook offers a view of rural scenery nestled in a narrow valley. The Chestnut Ridge Overlook provides access to the 5.4-mile Chestnut Ridge Loop Trail. The Roanoke Mountain Campground (closed during the winter) is located 1.5 miles off the Parkway and provides primitive campsites with tables and grills for tents, trailers, and motor homes.

A short distance beyond the campground is the Mill Mountain Zoological Park and Wildflower Garden. The 10-acre zoo exhibits more than forty-five species of exotic and native animals. The facilities, in partnership with Explore Park, are devoted to breeding endangered species of North American flora and fauna.

The short walk from the parking area to the zoo is made more pleasurable by passing through the Wildflower Garden, where many Appalachian mountain wildflowers are to be found. The wildflowers listed below were found growing at the overlooks along the spur road and do not include those in the Wildflower Garden.

SPRING
Field Pansy
Kidneyleaf Buttercup
Common Winter Cress
Flowering Dogwood
Dwarf Cinquefoil
Blackberry
Yellow Wood Sorrel
Hop Clover
Plantain-leaved
  Pussytoes
Common Fleabane
Tall Buttercup
Garlic Mustard
Cleavers
Mouse-ear Hawkweed

SUMMER
Mouse-ear Hawkweed
Common Cinquefoil
Hop Clover
Queen Anne's Lace
Ox-eye Daisy
Daisy Fleabane
Yarrow
Yellow Sweet Clover
Japanese Honeysuckle
Yellow Goat's-beard
Common Milkweed
Crown Vetch
Horse-nettle
Spotted Knapweed
Flowering Spurge

Woolly Mullein
Black-eyed Susan
Field Thistle

FALL
Yellow Wood Sorrel
Black-eyed Susan
Field Thistle
Crown-beard
Horse-nettle
Spotted Knapweed
Goldenrods
White-flowered Asters

Miles 129–130

*Roanoke Valley, Lost Mountain,
and Poages Mill Views* Elevation: 2,200'

These overlooks are closely grouped, and each has an excellent view to the northeast, over the Roanoke Valley and the city of Roanoke, Virginia. During mid-May the view is graced by a number of tall Princess trees covered with bright blue, tubular blossoms. During all seasons the lights of Roanoke provide a spectacular nighttime view. The name "Roanoke" comes from the Indian word for "money," which consisted of seashells gathered along the tidewater regions of Virginia and North Carolina. At the Lost Mountain View, Lost Mountain is visible in the northwest, rising to an elevation of 2,160 feet.

If you are here early in the spring, look for the shepherd's-purse, easy to identify by its small, purse-like seedpods.

SPRING
Shepherd's-purse
Common Winter Cress
Yellow Wood Sorrel
Dwarf Cinquefoil
Blackberry
Flowering Dogwood
Wild Geranium
King Devil
Common Buttercup
Crested Dwarf Iris
Great Laurel

SUMMER
Yellow Wood Sorrel
King Devil
Hop Clover

Mouse-ear Hawkweed
White Campion
Japanese Honeysuckle
Mountain Laurel
Bladder Campion
Bowman's-root
Yarrow
Deptford Pink
Smooth Hawk's-beard
White Sweet Clover
Queen Anne's Lace
Southern Harebell
Chicory
Heal-all
Greater Coreopsis
Spotted Knapweed
Poke Milkweed

Woolly Mullein
Hedge Bindweed
Bull Thistle
Pale Touch-me-not
White-flowered Asters

FALL
Yellow Wood Sorrel
White-flowered Asters
Hedge Bindweed
Queen Anne's Lace
Spotted Touch-me-not
Bull Thistle
Spotted Knapweed
White Campion
Goldenrods
White Snakeroot

Mile 139

Cahas Mountain View Elevation: 3,013'

Cahas Mountain, rising to an elevation of 3,571 feet, is the peak off to the left of the overlook. The name "cahas" is thought to have come from the Totero Indian word *kihi*, meaning "crow." Apparently the Toteros were a seminomadic tribe, and many of their relics have been found on or near Cahas Mountain.

This view has an excellent variety of summer wildflowers. See if you can find the spotted bracts of the spotted knapweed.

SPRING
Purple Dead Nettle
Wild Strawberry

Common Blue Violet
Field Pansy
Flowering Dogwood

Dwarf Cinquefoil
Blackberry
Common Winter Cress

Common Fleabane	King Devil	Hoary Tick-trefoil
Mouse-ear Hawkweed	Yarrow	
	Queen Anne's Lace	FALL
SUMMER	White Avens	Queen Anne's Lace
Blackberry	English Plantain	Heal-all
Mouse-ear Hawkweed	Lance-leaved Coreopsis	Yellow Wood Sorrel
Hop Clover	Heal-all	White Campion
White Campion	Spotted Knapweed	Spotted Knapweed
Bladder Campion	Green-headed	Whorled Rosinweed
Common Cinquefoil	Coneflower	Goldenrods
Daisy Fleabane	Yellow Wood Sorrel	White-flowered Asters

Mile 154.1

Smart View Overlook Elevation: 2,564'

This overlook, bordered by a rustic, split-rail fence, looks out over a long, low valley in Franklin County, Virginia. A nearby "people's gate" in the fence provides access to the 2.6-mile Smart View loop hiking trail. The Smart View Picnic Area at Mile 154.6 also provides access to the trail and features a selection of open and wooded picnic sites.

In early fall, see if you can find the upland boneset that grows here. This tall member of the thoroughwort family is crowned by a cluster of fuzzy flowers and has slender, pointed, stalkless leaves. This plant was valued by early medical practitioners as a cure for a wide range of ailments, including bone-break fever.

SPRING	SUMMER	Goldenrods
Henbit	Mouse-ear Hawkweed	Spotted Knapweed
Purple Dead Nettle	Hop Clover	Pigeonberry
Shepherd's-purse	Common Cinquefoil	Heal-all
Bird's-eye Speedwell	King Devil	Southern Harebell
Hairy Bitter Cress	Blackberry	Wing-stem
Wild Strawberry	White Campion	Upland Boneset
Common Blue Violet	Yellow Wood Sorrel	
Flowering Dogwood	Yarrow	FALL
Common Fleabane	Daisy Fleabane	Queen Anne's Lace
Common Winter Cress	Crown Vetch	Spotted Knapweed
Dwarf Cinquefoil	Lance-leaved Coreopsis	Daisy Fleabane
Mouse-ear Chickweed	Queen Anne's Lace	Yellow Wood Sorrel
Spring Vetch	Fringed Loosestrife	Upland Boneset

Field Thistle
Whorled Rosinweed
Crown-beard

White Snakeroot
Long-bristled
Smartweed

White-flowered Asters
Goldenrods

Mile 162.4
✿ Rakes Mill Pond

This clear, cool pond was created by a stone-faced dam built in the early nineteenth century by a miller named Jarmon Rakes. While the dam is still in place, the Rakes grist mill has long since disappeared. Folks waiting for Jarmon to grind their corn fished for trout in the pond. Lucky ones took home a mess of fish along with their cornmeal. Steps lead to a rustic stone patio at the pond's edge.

Many of the wildflowers listed below can be found by walking along the pond's edge. For a special treat, look for the larger blue flag iris in the early summer.

SPRING
Skunk Cabbage
Kidneyleaf Buttercup
Gill-over-the-ground
Wild Strawberry
Early Winter Cress
Common Blue Violet
Hooked Buttercup
Giant Chickweed
Cleavers
Common Fleabane

SUMMER
Blackberry
Yarrow
Hop Clover
Mouse-ear Hawkweed
Golden Alexander
Larger Blue Flag Iris
Common Cinquefoil

King Devil
Large Houstonia
Crown Vetch
Hollow Joe-pye-weed
Water Hemlock
Common Milkweed
Queen Anne's Lace
Black-eyed Susan
Yellow Wood Sorrel
Lance-leaved Coreopsis
Horse-nettle
Greater Coreopsis
Ox-eye Daisy
Poke Milkweed
Whorled Rosinweed
Spotted Touch-me-not
Evening Primrose
Hedge Bindweed
Heal-all

Green-headed
  Coneflower
Pale Indian-plantain
Spotted Knapweed
Southern Harebell

FALL
Queen Anne's Lace
Black-eyed Susan
Hedge Bindweed
Yellow Wood Sorrel
Hollow Joe-pye-weed
New York Ironweed
Common Sneeze-weed
Blue-flowered Asters
Arrow-leaf Tearthumb
Wild Bean
Goldenrods
White-flowered Asters

Mile 168

The Saddle

This overlook is situated in a saddle-like depression in the ridge line connecting two high points of Rocky Knob mountain. The view to the east is over Rock Castle Gorge with Sugarloaf Mountain in the distance. The Rock Castle Gorge Trail, which can be entered here, leads down into the gorge to Rock Castle Creek.

One of the Parkway's more common wildflowers, yarrow, blooms here during the summer and fall. Look for its clusters of creamy white flowers and feathery leaves.

SPRING
Gill-over-the-ground
Bloodroot
Common Blue Violet
Wild Strawberry
Garlic Mustard
Giant Chickweed
Large-flowered
   Trillium
Hispid Buttercup
Dwarf Cinquefoil

SUMMER
Yellow Wood Sorrel
Mouse-ear Hawkweed
False Solomon's-seal
Spiderwort
King Devil
Bowman's-root
Common Milkweed
Hedge Bindweed
Spotted Knapweed
Yarrow

Greater Coreopsis
Southern Harebell

FALL
Southern Harebell
Hedge Bindweed
Yarrow
Queen Anne's Lace
Common Sneeze-weed
Goldenrods
White-flowered Asters

Mile 176.2

Mabry Mill

This picturesque old mill and water wheel is without a doubt the most photographed site on the Blue Ridge Parkway. The mill, actually a sawmill and blacksmith shop, was operated by E. B. Mabry from 1910 until 1935. Nearby and around the mill is a self-guided tour of old-time mountain industries, a coffee shop (closed during the winter), and a large picnic area.

Wildflowers here are abundant along the trails and around the mill pond.

SPRING
Skunk Cabbage
Gill-over-the-ground
Common Blue Violet
Kidneyleaf Buttercup

Wild Strawberry
Common Winter Cress
Red Trillium
Flowering Dogwood
Wood Anemone

Smooth Rock-cress
May-apple
Garlic Mustard
Painted Trillium

SUMMER
Yellow Wood Sorrel
Mountain Laurel
Bladder Campion
Daisy Fleabane
White Avens
Great Laurel
Thimbleweed
Heal-all
Hollow Joe-pye-weed
Evening Primrose
Pale Touch-me-not

Queen Anne's Lace
Water Hemlock
Green-headed
  Coneflower
White Snakeroot
Wing-stem

FALL
Queen Anne's Lace
Hollow Joe-pye-weed
Spotted Touch-me-not

Green-headed
  Coneflower
Wing-stem
Hyssop-leaved Boneset
Common Sneeze-weed
Crown-beard
Goldenrods
Whorled Rosinweed
White Snakeroot
Arrow-leaf Tearthumb
Blue-flowered Asters

Mile 179.3

❀ *Round Meadow Overlook and Trail* Elevation: 2,800'

This overlook is located just above Round Meadow Creek and provides access to the Round Meadow Creek Trail, a leisurely 20-minute walk. Round Meadow Creek joins Mayberry Creek a few miles from this spot, then flows on through Townes Dam and finally empties into the Dan River in Kibler Valley.

Many of this overlook's spring wildflowers will be found along the trail. Watch especially for red trillium with its rare salmon-colored blossoms.

SPRING
Gill-over-the-ground
Wild Strawberry
Kidneyleaf Buttercup
Early Winter Cress
Common Blue Violet
Dwarf Cinquefoil
Giant Chickweed
Sweet White Violet
Smooth Rock-cress
Common Buttercup
Red Trillium
Wood Anemone
Solomon's Seal
Flowering Dogwood
Common Winter Cress
Garlic Mustard
Painted Trillium

Mouse-ear Chickweed
Common Cinquefoil
Hooked Buttercup
Common Fleabane

SUMMER
Blackberry
Mountain Laurel
Yellow Wood Sorrel
Yarrow
Horse-nettle
Daisy Fleabane
Ox-eye Daisy
Great Laurel
Lance-leaved Coreopsis
Common St. John's-
  wort
Common Milkweed

Sweet Cicely
Heal-all
Queen Anne's Lace
Evening Primrose
Indian Pipe
Virgin's Bower
White Snakeroot

FALL
Horse-nettle
Yellow Wood Sorrel
Queen Anne's Lace
Hollow Joe-pye-weed
Spotted Joe-pye-weed
White-flowered Asters

Common Sneeze-weed	White Snakeroot	Long-bristled
Bull Thistle	Blue-flowered Asters	Smartweed
Crown-beard	Goldenrods	

Mile 189.1

Pilot Mountain View Elevation: 2,950'

Pilot Mountain, near Mount Airy, North Carolina, is visible 25 miles in the distance. This isolated peak is a survivor of an ancient mountain range that has eroded away over the centuries. Pilot Mountain stands 1,500 feet above the surrounding countryside and served as a landmark for Indians and early settlers. The mountain was called *Jomeokee* by the Indians, meaning "the Great Guide." It has also been known in the past as "Stonehead" (1753) and as "Mount Ararat" (1770). It became known as Pilot Mountain in the early days of aviation, when it served as a landmark for pilots.

Bird's-eye speedwell blooms here early in the spring. Take a close look at the blossom. Does it remind you of a bird's eye?

SPRING	Mouse-ear Hawkweed	Common Milkweed
Wild Strawberry	Golden Ragwort	Yellow Wood Sorrel
Golden Ragwort	English Plantain	
Early Winter Cress	Golden Alexander	FALL
Flowering Dogwood	Daisy Fleabane	Daisy Fleabane
Common Cinquefoil	Yarrow	Spotted Knapweed
Golden Alexander	Ox-eye Daisy	Common Milkweed
Bulbous Buttercup	Black-eyed Susan	Black-eyed Susan
Common Fleabane	Queen Anne's Lace	Queen Anne's Lace
Lyre-leaved Sage	Spotted Knapweed	Heal-all
	Heal-all	Lance-leaved Coreopsis
SUMMER	Lance-leaved Coreopsis	Yellow Wood Sorrel
Bird's-eye Speedwell	Evening Primrose	Goldenrods
Hop Clover		White-flowered Asters

Mile 218.7

High Piney Spur and Fox Hunter's Paradise Overlook

There are two parking areas here. One features a Park Service exhibit that describes Fox Hunter's Paradise; the other provides access to a short trail to a beautiful mountainside overlook surrounded by a rock wall. Early one cool spring morning, I found two empty champagne glasses placed carefully side by side on the rock wall. I often wonder about the couple who the night before shared a wonderful moment of celebration on that beautiful spot. From this overlook it is not difficult to imagine fox hunters of old, huddled around a campfire in the woods below, spinning tales of the day's hunt.

Many of the wildflowers here are woodland species that can be found along the trail and around the edge of the wooded parking area.

SPRING
Kidneyleaf Buttercup
Common Blue Violet
Wild Strawberry
Dwarf Cinquefoil
Gill-over-the-ground
Flowering Dogwood
Common Winter Cress
Golden Ragwort
Blackberry
Giant Chickweed
Solomon's Seal
Pinxter-flower
Bowman's-root
Flame Azalea
Wild Geranium

Yellow Star-grass
Common Fleabane
False Solomon's-seal
Plantain-leaved
   Pussytoes

SUMMER
Bowman's-root
False Solomon's-seal
Yarrow
Greater Coreopsis
Thimbleweed
Spiderwort
Daisy Fleabane
Common St. John's-
   wort

Lance-leaved Coreopsis
Upland Boneset
Heal-all
White Snakeroot
Goldenrods

FALL
Yellow Wood Sorrel
White-flowered Asters
Lance-leaved Coreopsis
Goldenrods
Upland Boneset
White Snakeroot
Silverrod

Mile 230.1
❀ *Little Glade Mill Pond* Elevation: 2,709'

There are no spectacular views of ridges and valleys here at the Little Glade Mill Pond, yet this is one of the most beautiful and tranquil settings on the Parkway. The old mill pond is fed by the cold, rushing waters of a mountain stream, and around the pond, well spaced for privacy, are numerous quiet and shaded picnic tables. This is a perfect spot to pause for a picnic lunch or just to rest and relax.

If you're looking for wildflowers, walk along Little Glade Creek, which flows along the forested rim of the picnic area.

SPRING
Skunk Cabbage
Bluets
Wild Strawberry
Bulbous Buttercup
Common Blue Violet
Common Chickweed
Common Cinquefoil
Common Fleabane
Common Winter Cress
Dwarf Cinquefoil
Flowering Dogwood
Hispid Buttercup
Lyre-leaved Sage
Wood Anemone

SUMMER
Asiatic Dayflower
Blackberry
Boneset

Common Cinquefoil
English Plantain
Heal-all
Hoary Mountain Mint
Hollow Joe-pye-weed
Japanese Honeysuckle
Larger Blue Flag Iris
Lance-leaved Coreopsis
Lesser Stitchwort
Meadow-sweet
Mountain Laurel
Ox-eye Daisy
Pale Touch-me-not
Great Laurel
Shrubby St. John's-wort
Smooth Hawk's-beard
Spotted Touch-me-not
Swamp Rose
Virgin's Bower
Yarrow

FALL
Arrow-leaf Tearthumb
Blue-flowered Asters
Boneset
Evening Primrose
Goldenrods
Heal-all
Hollow Joe-pye-weed
Horse-nettle
Lance-leaved Coreopsis
New York Ironweed
Rattlesnake-root
Smooth Hawk's-beard
Spotted Touch-me-not
Virgin's Bower
White Snakeroot
Yellow Wood Sorrel

Mile 232.5

Stone Mountain Overlook Elevation: 3,115'

This overlook faces almost due south. Clearly visible in the distance is Stone Mountain, a 600-foot-high, oval-shaped mass of light gray granite. The geology of Stone Mountain is explained by a nearby Park Service exhibit. Stone Mountain State Park, which can be reached by driving east on Route 21 from Milepost 229, is a major tourist attraction in this area.

Many of the wildflowers here are on the rocky embankment behind the overlook.

SPRING
Bluets
Common Blue Violet
Wild Strawberry
Common Winter Cress
Dwarf Cinquefoil
Flowering Dogwood
Yellow Wood Sorrel
Mouse-ear Hawkweed
Blackberry

Common Cinquefoil
Plantain-leaved
    Pussytoes
Lyre-leaved Sage
Cat's-ear

SUMMER
Hop Clover
Mouse-ear Hawkweed
Cat's-ear

Daisy Fleabane
Mountain Laurel
Smooth Hawk's-beard
King Devil
Small's Ragwort
Yarrow
Ox-eye Daisy
Hoary Mountain Mint
Fringed Loosestrife
Yellow Wood Sorrel

Horse-nettle	Southern Harebell	Southern Harebell
Great Laurel	Heal-all	Horse-nettle
Flowering Spurge	Woodland Sunflower	Maryland Golden
Lance-leaved Coreopsis	Maryland Golden	Aster
Asiatic Dayflower	Aster	Woodland Sunflower
Woolly Mullein	White Snakeroot	Lance-leaved Coreopsis
English Plantain		Black-eyed Susan
Common St. John's-	FALL	White Snakeroot
wort	Heal-all	Goldenrods
Pale Touch-me-not	Yellow Wood Sorrel	Tall Sunflower

Mile 235

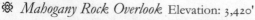 *Mahogany Rock Overlook* Elevation: 3,420'

The view from the Mahogany Rock Overlook is across a wide valley to the north. The town of Sparta, North Carolina, home of Dr. Graybow's Pre-smoked Pipes company, is visible in the distance. The line of ridges across the valley is the Peach Bottom mountain range. Back to the east-northeast and across the Parkway is nearby Mahogany Rock Mountain. At one time, a cable car carried sightseers from the top of Mahogany Rock Mountain to Scott's Ridge, which is the nearby ridge to the southeast. To the east is an excellent view of Stone Mountain.

This overlook is a monitoring point for the annual fall migration of birds of prey. From early September to late November, thousands of hawks, eagles, and vultures migrate southward past this point.

Many of the wildflowers here will be found along the east side of the stone wall on the Mahogany Rock Mountain side of the Parkway.

SPRING	Plantain-leaved	Mountain Laurel
Bluets	Pussytoes	New Jersey Tea
Wild Strawberry	Squaw-huckleberry	Mouse-ear Hawkweed
Common Blue Violet	King Devil	Smooth Hawk's-beard
Common Winter Cress	Golden Ragwort	Yarrow
Dwarf Cinquefoil		Deptford Pink
Flowering Dogwood	SUMMER	Yellow Wood Sorrel
Kidneyleaf Buttercup	Wild Strawberry	English Plantain
Large Houstonia	King Devil	Lance-leaved Coreopsis
Blackberry	Dwarf Cinquefoil	Ox-eye Daisy
Early Meadow Rue	Daisy Fleabane	Whorled Loosestrife
Mouse-ear Hawkweed	Mouse-ear Chickweed	Heal-all

Bladder Campion	FALL	Field Thistle
Great Laurel	Horse-nettle	White Snakeroot
Evening Primrose	Yellow Wood Sorrel	Pigeonberry
Southern Harebell	Spotted Knapweed	Goldenrods
Spotted Knapweed	Southern Harebell	Pale Indian-plantain
Virgin's Bower	Virgin's Bower	Leather Flower
	New Jersey Tea	Horse-nettle
	Lance-leaved Coreopsis	Wild Basil

Mile 236.9

Air Bellows Overlook Elevation: 3,428'

Air Bellows Overlook faces north-northwest, where the Peach Bottom Mountains can be seen in the distance. At your feet lies a long valley dotted with dairy farms, Christmas-tree farms, and summer homes. Visible about five miles to the north is the town of Sparta, North Carolina. If you happen to be here when a strong wind is blowing from the north, you'll know why this overlook is called "Air Bellows."

Many of the wildflowers here will be found at the base of the cliff behind the overlook.

SPRING	Lesser Stitchwort	Goldenrods
Bluets	Mountain Laurel	Evening Primrose
Common Blue Violet	Yarrow	Spotted Touch-me-not
Wild Strawberry	Ox-eye Daisy	Queen Anne's Lace
Common Winter Cress	Lance-leaved Coreopsis	
Giant Chickweed	Smooth Hawk's-beard	FALL
Dwarf Cinquefoil	Great Laurel	Yellow Wood Sorrel
Flowering Dogwood	Thimbleweed	Evening Primrose
Yellow Wood Sorrel	Daisy Fleabane	Spotted Touch-me-not
Crested Dwarf Iris	Whorled Loosestrife	Goldenrods
Plantain-leaved	Yellow Wood Sorrel	Queen Anne's Lace
Pussytoes	Heal-all	Virgin's Bower
Common Cinquefoil	Common St. John's-	Spotted Knapweed
	wort	White-flowered Asters
SUMMER	Spotted Knapweed	White Snakeroot
Bluets	Virgin's Bower	Black-eyed Susan
King Devil	Hedge Bindweed	Hedge Bindweed
Mouse-ear Hawkweed	Pale Touch-me-not	Lance-leaved Coreopsis
Blackberry	White-flowered Asters	Silverrod

Mile 240.9

Doughton Park Overlook

This overlook is only a short distance off the Parkway, near the Doughton Park Restaurant and Service Station. It is not as heavily visited as some of the Parkway's other overlooks, but the unobstructed panoramic views to the north and west make this a worthwhile stop.

Another reason to stop is the multitude of wildflowers growing in the fields around the overlook and along a nearby hiking trail that leads across open pastures.

SPRING
Bluets
Common Blue Violet
Wild Strawberry
Common Winter Cress
Dwarf Cinquefoil
Golden Ragwort
Common Cinquefoil
Blackberry
Yellow Wood Sorrel
Sweet White Violet
May-apple

SUMMER
Mouse-ear Hawkweed
Lesser Stitchwort
King Devil
Common Cinquefoil
Blackberry

Smooth Hawk's-beard
Horse-nettle
Yellow Wood Sorrel
Yarrow
Ox-eye Daisy
Great Laurel
Asiatic Dayflower
Deptford Pink
Golden Ragwort
English Plantain
Black-eyed Susan
Hoary Mountain Mint
Queen Anne's Lace
Common Milkweed
Heal-all
Spotted Knapweed
Lance-leaved Coreopsis
Common Sneeze-weed
Field Thistle

Bull Thistle

FALL
Heal-all
Black-eyed Susan
Queen Anne's Lace
Horse-nettle
Yellow Wood Sorrel
Crown Vetch
Hoary Mountain Mint
Lance-leaved Coreopsis
Field Thistle
Bull Thistle
Common Sneeze-weed
Goldenrods
White Snakeroot
Spotted Knapweed
White-flowered Asters
Silverrod

Mile 242.3

Alligator Back Elevation: 3,385'

Alligator Back is so named because the view of distant mountains puts one in mind of the bumpy profile of an alligator's back. A rock-walled overlook provides a wonderful view of a deep gorge, which snakes its way off to the southeast. Across the Parkway are equally impressive views of distant mountain ranges and lush valleys.

Alligator Back is also a parking area for hikers wishing to access the Bluff Mountain Trail. The trail to the Bluff Mountain Overlook is about one mile long and rises to an elevation of 3,800 feet. This is not an especially strenuous trail for hikers who are in good physical condition; for those who are not, it could prove difficult. However, the view from the overlook is well worth the climb.

This is one of the best locations on the Parkway for finding the elusive bird-foot violet. Look for it in the grassy areas along the trail to the nearby rock formations. During the fall months, several species of fall asters can be found in the same area.

SPRING	SUMMER	FALL
Bluets	Yellow Wood Sorrel	Horse-nettle
Wild Strawberry	Daisy Fleabane	Maryland Golden
Common Blue Violet	Mountain Laurel	Aster
Field Pansy	Yarrow	Heal-all
Dwarf Cinquefoil	Smooth Hawk's-beard	Evening Primrose
Common Winter Cress	Whorled Loosestrife	Lance-leaved Coreopsis
Bird-foot Violet	Horse-nettle	Goldenrods
Common Cinquefoil	Ox-eye Daisy	Field Thistle
Golden Ragwort	English Plantain	Blue-flowered Asters
Yellow Wood Sorrel	Hoary Mountain Mint	White Snakeroot

Mile 252.8

Sheets Gap Overlook Elevation: 3,342'

This loop drive overlook has a panoramic view to the east that sweeps from north to south. The view encompasses folding mountains and valleys as far as the eye can see. Around 1815, Jess Sheets built a cabin in the nearby gap, and several generations of the Sheets family lived there until the property was sold for the construction of the Parkway.

Several picnic tables are available here for a quiet picnic lunch, and the unmowed meadow in front of the overlook is filled with wildflowers. If you visit here during late June or early July, look for the whorled loosestrife. More of it can be found here than at any other site on the Parkway.

SPRING	SUMMER	
Bluets	Bluets	Horse-nettle
Wild Strawberry	Mouse-ear Hawkweed	Wild Basil
Common Blue Violet	Yellow Wood Sorrel	Evening Primrose
Common Cinquefoil	Blackberry	Catnip
Early Winter Cress	Solomon's Seal	Virgin's Bower
Flowering Dogwood	Yarrow	Common Milkweed
Dwarf Cinquefoil	Small's Ragwort	Hoary Mountain Mint
Crested Dwarf Iris	Ox-eye Daisy	White-flowered Asters
Plantain-leaved	King Devil	
Pussytoes	Smooth Hawk's-beard	FALL
Common Fleabane	Common Cinquefoil	Heal-all
Golden Ragwort	Hedge Bindweed	Horse-nettle
Common Winter Cress	Queen Anne's Lace	Lance-leaved Coreopsis
Blackberry	English Plantain	Southern Harebell
Goat's Rue	Great Laurel	White Snakeroot
Yellow Wood Sorrel	Whorled Loosestrife	White-flowered Asters
Mouse-ear Chickweed	Thimbleweed	Virgin's Bower
Solomon's Seal	Heal-all	Goldenrods

Mile 260.3

Jumpinoff Rocks Overlook Elevation: 3,165'

The half-mile trail from the parking area to Jumpinoff Rocks is a quiet, cool passage through mountain laurel, great laurel, and trailing arbutus. Carpets of lush, green galax cover the ground, and spring and summer wildflowers are in abundance. Jumpinoff Rocks is perched high on the edge of a bowl-like depression known as Middle Creek Valley. The origin of the name "Jumpinoff Rocks" is unclear. However, it is something you would definitely not want to do.

SPRING		
Common Blue Violet	Squaw-root	Bowman's-root
Giant Chickweed	Common Fleabane	Giant Chickweed
Halberd-leaved Violet	Blackberry	Mouse-ear Hawkweed
Golden Ragwort	Flame Azalea	King Devil
Round-leaved Violet	False Solomon's-seal	Great Laurel
Kidneyleaf Buttercup	Solomon's Seal	Yellow Wood Sorrel
Wild Strawberry		Poke Milkweed
Pinxter-flower	SUMMER	Daisy Fleabane
Golden Alexander	Mountain Laurel	Bluets
Mountain Bellwort	Solomon's Seal	Heal-all
	Galax	Wild Bergamot

Virgin's Bower
Pale Touch-me-not
Sweet Joe-pye-weed
Goldenrods

FALL
Yellow Wood Sorrel
Flowering Spurge
Virgin's Bower
Heal-all
Pale Touch-me-not

White-flowered Asters
Goldenrods
Silverrod
White Snakeroot
Rattlesnake-root

Mile 272
❀ *The Cascades Parking Area and Trail*

Clear mountain air, a beautiful view of distant mountains beyond a deep valley, the sweet scent of pine needles, and shaded tables create a pastoral scene for a leisurely picnic lunch. After lunch, take a hike on the 30-minute round-trip trail through an evergreen maze of mountain laurel and great laurel to the Cascades of Falls Creek. The creek runs parallel to the trail for a short distance, then suddenly and dramatically cascades down a slick spillway. Along the trail look for the spectacular springtime flame azalea, the early-summer galax, and the early-fall pale touch-me-not.

As if all this were not enough, restrooms are conveniently located nearby.

SPRING
Common Blue Violet
Wild Strawberry
Bird's-eye Speedwell
Dwarf Cinquefoil
Kidneyleaf Buttercup
Common Winter Cress
Gill-over-the-ground
Flowering Dogwood
Golden Ragwort
Hooked Buttercup
Blackberry
Giant Chickweed
Flame Azalea
Common Fleabane
Mountain Bellwort

Solomon's Seal
Mountain Laurel

SUMMER
Blackberry
Mountain Laurel
Mouse-ear Hawkweed
Solomon's Seal
Galax
Black Cohosh
Heal-all
Thimbleweed
Ox-eye Daisy
Smooth Hawk's-beard
Yellow Wood Sorrel
Great Laurel

Greater Coreopsis
Pale Touch-me-not
Lance-leaved Coreopsis
Goldenrods
Pale Indian-plantain

FALL
Pale Touch-me-not
Yellow Wood Sorrel
Goldenrods
Heal-all
Sweet Joe-pye-weed
White-flowered Asters
Wing-stem
White Snakeroot
Blue-flowered Asters

Mile 277.9

Osborne Mountain View Elevation: 3,200'

This overlook offers a clear view of Osborne Mountain, the high point of the ridge directly in front of the overlook. In late spring and early summer, nearly twenty species of wildflowers blanket the slope between the parking area and the tree line.

SPRING
Purple Dead Nettle
Bird's-eye Speedwell
Early Winter Cress
Common Blue Violet
Wild Strawberry
Common Cinquefoil
Common Buttercup
Mouse-ear Chickweed
Dwarf Cinquefoil
Common Fleabane
Plantain-leaved
  Pussytoes
Lyre-leaved Sage
Tufted Vetch

SUMMER
Wild Strawberry
Hairy Hawkweed
Common Cinquefoil
Hop Clover
Mouse-ear Hawkweed
Blue-eyed Grass
Lesser Stitchwort
Large Houstonia
Queen Anne's Lace
Heal-all
Flowering Spurge
Daisy Fleabane
Hoary Mountain Mint
Horse-nettle
Ox-eye Daisy
Whorled Coreopsis
Black-eyed Susan

Deptford Pink
Maryland Golden
  Aster
Goldenrods

FALL
Horse-nettle
Whorled Loosestrife
Heal-all
Queen Anne's Lace
Deptford Pink
Maryland Golden
  Aster
Goldenrods
Field Thistle
Blue-flowered Asters
Wandlike Bush-Clover

Mile 281.5

Grandview Overlook Elevation: 3,240'

This really is a grand view of the southeast corner of Watauga County, North Carolina, formed in 1849 and named for the Watauga River. The name Watauga is from the Indian word meaning "beautiful water."

A stretch of the unmowed pasture below this overlook is a virtual wildflower garden. By the end of June it is filled with heal-all, ox-eye daisy, daisy fleabane, and more.

SPRING
Wild Strawberry
Common Blue Violet
Bird's-eye Speedwell
Gill-over-the-ground

Common Winter Cress
Flowering Dogwood
Common Fleabane
Blackberry
False Solomon's-seal

SUMMER
Wild Strawberry
Common Blue Violet
False Solomon's-seal
Blackberry

Smooth Hawk's-beard
Mouse-ear Hawkweed
Hairy Hawkweed
Common Speedwell
Yarrow
Daisy Fleabane
Common Cinquefoil
Lesser Stitchwort
Blue-eyed Grass
Heal-all
Ox-eye Daisy
Yellow Wood Sorrel
Common Milkweed
Queen Anne's Lace
English Plantain

Horse-nettle
Flowering Spurge
Virgin's Bower
Goldenrods
Wild Blue Phlox
Pale Touch-me-not
Chicory
Deptford Pink
Hedge Bindweed
Rough-fruited
   Cinquefoil

FALL
Yellow Wood Sorrel
Heal-all

Virgin's Bower
Pale Touch-me-not
Spotted Touch-me-not
White-flowered Asters
Flowering Spurge
Horse-nettle
Wandlike Bush-Clover
Wing-stem
White Snakeroot
Hoary Tick-trefoil
Goldenrods
Blue-flowered Asters

Mile 289.6

Raven Rock Overlook Elevation: 3,810'

This overlook is situated on an outcrop known as Raven Rock. It is quite possible that at one time or another ravens may have roosted here, because they are common in the area. The large, black birds (larger than a crow) can best be identified by their guttural voice, which reminds one of an old man clearing his throat.

Many of the wildflowers here grow among the rocks just beyond the split-rail fence.

SPRING
Bird's-eye Speedwell
Giant Chickweed
Early Winter Cress
Gill-over-the-ground
Common Cinquefoil
Common Blue Violet
Mouse-ear Chickweed
Mountain Bellwort
Smooth Rock-cress
Lily of the Valley
Solomon's Seal

SUMMER
Yarrow

Mountain Laurel
Hairy Hawkweed
Common Cinquefoil
Spiderwort
Large Houstonia
Whorled Loosestrife
Lesser Stitchwort
Small's Beard-tongue
English Plantain
Daisy Fleabane
Great Laurel
Ox-eye Daisy
Pale Touch-me-not
Evening Primrose
Southern Harebell

Heal-all
Peruvian Daisy
Virgin's Bower

FALL
Peruvian Daisy
Virgin's Bower
Heal-all
Pale Touch-me-not
Hoary Tick-trefoil
Goldenrods
White-flowered Asters
White Snakeroot
Blue-flowered Asters
Silverrod

Mile 290.5
Thunder Hill Overlook Elevation: 3,795'

The Thunder Hill Overlook provides an excellent view down into the Yadkin Valley, where the headwaters of the Yadkin River are formed. The Yadkin River flows to the southeast and is eventually joined by the Uwharrie River. Together they form the Pee Dee River, which flows on to the South Carolina coast, where it empties into Winyah Bay.

Many of this overlook's wildflowers inhabit the embankment below the parking area as well as the open fields across the Parkway. A "people's gate" in the fence provides access to the fields.

SPRING
Common Blue Violet
Wild Strawberry
Bird's-eye Speedwell
Common Winter Cress
Purple Dead Nettle
Flowering Dogwood
Mouse-ear Chickweed
Blackberry
Common Cinquefoil

SUMMER
Blackberry
Common Cinquefoil

Yellow Wood Sorrel
Smooth Hawk's-beard
Spiderwort
Blue-eyed Grass
Common Buttercup
Daisy Fleabane
Heal-all
English Plantain
Horse-nettle
Deptford Pink
Yarrow
Pale Touch-me-not
Southern Harebell

Ox-eye Daisy
Virgin's Bower

FALL
Yellow Wood Sorrel
Virgin's Bower
Heal-all
Yarrow
Pale Touch-me-not
Goldenrods
Horse-nettle
White-flowered Asters
White Snakeroot

Mile 294
❀ *Moses Cone Manor and Craft Shop*

The Moses Cone Manor and Craft Shop, formerly known as Flat Top Manor, was the summer estate of Moses H. Cone, a textile executive from Greensboro, North Carolina. The manor now serves as a museum and has a unique craft shop operated by the Southern Highland Handicraft Guild, whose members conduct periodic craft-making demonstrations. The surrounding area is crisscrossed by hiking trails, and a bridle path passes the front of the manor.

The easy-to-walk Figure 8 Trail behind the manor is an excellent spot to look for spring and summer wildflowers.

SPRING	SUMMER	Woolly Mullein
Bird's-eye Speedwell	Mountain Laurel	Evening Primrose
Common Blue Violet	Common Buttercup	
Crested Dwarf Iris	Spiderwort	FALL
Dwarf Cinquefoil	Solomon's Seal	Bull Thistle
Kidneyleaf Buttercup	Large Houstonia	Common Burdock
Common Fleabane	Ox-eye Daisy	Pale Touch-me-not
Halberd-leaved Violet	Daisy Fleabane	Queen Anne's Lace
Painted Trillium	Smooth Hawk's-beard	Heal-all
Common Lousewort	Yarrow	Horse-nettle
Gill-over-the-ground	Pale Touch-me-not	Filmy Angelica
Golden Ragwort	Heal-all	Pigeonberry
Large Flowered	Bowman's-root	Starry Campion
Trillium	Deptford Pink	Common Sneeze-weed
Giant Chickweed	Yarrow	Yellow Wood Sorrel
Round-leaved Yellow	Poke Milkweed	Peruvian Daisy
Violet	Dame's Rocket	Blue-flowered Asters
Early Meadow Rue	Wild Bergamot	White-flowered Asters
Mountain Bellwort	Whorled Loosestrife	White Snakeroot
Hooked Buttercup	Galax	Rattlesnake-root
Jack-in-the-Pulpit	Turk's-cap Lily	Horse-Balm
Henbit	White Avens	Long-bristled
Solomon's Seal	Horse-nettle	Smartweed
Common Winter Cress	Common Milkweed	
Hispid Buttercup	Queen Anne's Lace	
Blackberry	Greater Coreopsis	

Mile 301.8

Pilot Ridge Overlook Elevation: 4,400'

This overlook is located on Pilot Ridge, long and steep-sided, extending from the base of Grandfather Mountain to Calloway Peak. The view to the left of the overlook is down into the Globe, a huge hollow named by Bishop Spangenberg, the founder of the Moravian Church in America. There is a Pilot Ridge Road in the valley below, but it runs along the base of Backbone Ridge.

A number of wildflowers are to be found here, most on the steep slope behind the overlook.

SPRING	Dwarf Cinquefoil	Golden Ragwort
Bluets	Wild Strawberry	Common Fleabane
Common Winter Cress	Common Blue Violet	Mouse-ear Hawkweed

King Devil
Hop Clover

SUMMER
Bluets
Hop Clover
King Devil
Mountain Laurel
Blackberry
Yarrow
Daisy Fleabane
Ox-eye Daisy
Common Speedwell
Evening Primrose
Smooth Hawk's-beard
Heal-all
Black-eyed Susan
Deptford Pink
Queen Anne's Lace
Common Milkweed
Spotted Joe-pye-weed
Southern Harebell
Goldenrods
White-flowered Asters
White Snakeroot

FALL
White Snakeroot
Spotted Joe-pye-weed
Queen Anne's Lace
White-flowered Asters
Heal-all
Goldenrods

Mile 303.7

Wilson Creek Overlook Elevation: 4,357'

Wilson Creek crosses under the Parkway near the north entrance to this overlook and flows southeast to empty into the Johns River. Wildflowers here are highlighted by a large crop of midsummer crown vetch that covers the slope across the Parkway from the overlook.

SPRING
Bluets
Common Blue Violet
Common Winter Cress
Giant Chickweed
Mouse-ear Chickweed
Dwarf Cinquefoil
Creeping Buttercup
Sweet White Violet
Blackberry
Common Fleabane
False Solomon's-seal
King Devil

SUMMER
Blackberry
Hairy Hawkweed
Smooth Hawk's-beard
Crown Vetch
Blue-eyed Grass
Daisy Fleabane
Ox-eye Daisy
Yarrow
Heal-all
Pale Touch-me-not
Hop Clover
Rough-fruited Cinquefoil
Lesser Stitchwort
Love-vine
White Snakeroot
Evening Primrose

FALL
Heal-all
Evening Primrose
White Snakeroot
Pale Touch-me-not
White-flowered Asters
Nodding Ladies' Tresses
Goldenrods

Mile 304.7

❀ *Linn Cove Information Center and Trail*

This area features an information center and a number of Park Service exhibits. The Linn Cove Viaduct Observation Deck is located along the Tanawha Trail, just a short distance from the information center. This is an easy-to-walk trail that is lined with an abundance of wildflowers from early spring to late fall.

The Linn Cove Viaduct is part of the final 7.5-mile section of the Parkway completed in 1987. The viaduct, considered an engineering marvel, was constructed to avoid blasting away sections of revered Grandfather Mountain. The name "Linn Cove" is of Scottish origin. "Linn" refers to a craggy precipice or water falling down a steep mountainside, and a "cove" is a hollow in a rock formation.

During early summer, whorled loosestrife is abundant on the island surrounded by the parking area.

SPRING
Bluets
Bird's-eye Speedwell
Common Winter Cress
Red Trillium
Common Blue Violet
Pinxter-flower
Smooth Rock-cress
Hooked Buttercup
Painted Trillium
Golden Alexander
King Devil
Sweet White Violet
Lily of the Valley
Tall Meadow Rue
Blackberry
Umbrella-leaf

Solomon's Seal
May-apple

SUMMER
Blackberry
Smooth Hawk's-beard
Hairy Hawkweed
Bluets
Heal-all
Whorled Loosestrife
Shrubby St. John's-wort
Fly-Poison
Green-headed
   Coneflower
Daisy Fleabane
Evening Primrose
Crown Vetch

Woolly Mullein
Indian Pipe
White-flowered Asters
White Snakeroot
Spotted Touch-me-not
Lyon's Turtlehead
Love-vine

FALL
Evening Primrose
Spotted Touch-me-not
Love-vine
White Snakeroot
White-flowered Asters
Goldenrods

Mile 305 (Route 221)

Grandfather Mountain: Grandfather Overlook

Grandfather Mountain, with its Calloway Peak reaching an elevation of 5,964 feet, is the highest point on the Blue Ridge mountain range. The mountain has been thoughtfully developed into a top-rated natural attraction. Sixteen distinct habitats occur within the mountain's boundaries, with each habitat supporting a unique variety of plant and animal species. Several rare and endangered wildflower species, including Heller's Blazing Star and Gray's lily, are to be found here.

Visitors experience breathtaking views from Linville Peak, accessible by a mile-high, 228-foot-long, swinging footbridge. A nature museum broadens a visitor's interest in and association with nature through exhibits and movies. Some of the South's finest alpine trails are available for hiking and nature study. A small captive population of bear, deer, eagles, and cougar provide close encounters with some of the region's native birds and animals.

Grandfather Mountain is one mile west of the Parkway via Route 221, from the Linville exit at Mile 305. The Grandfather Overlook, which faces north over rolling mountains and valleys, is located along the road from the entrance to the summit of Grandfather Mountain.

A special springtime treat at the overlook is the wood strawberry, with its petite, white flowers arched above deep green leaves.

SPRING
Early Winter Cress
Gill-over-the-ground
Wood Strawberry
Common Cinquefoil
Dwarf Cinquefoil

SUMMER
Bluets
Hooked Buttercup

Pale Touch-me-not
Virgin's Bower
Yarrow
Blackberry
Creeping Buttercup
Yellow Wood Sorrel
Heal-all
Ox-eye Daisy
Daisy Fleabane
Southern Harebell

White-flowered Asters
White Snakeroot
Fringed Bindweed

FALL
Ox-eye Daisy
Heal-all
White Snakeroot
Blue-flowered Asters
Goldenrods

Mile 305 (Route 221)
Grandfather Mountain: Split Rock View

Like the Grandfather Overlook, this viewpoint is also located along the road from the entrance to the summit of Grandfather Mountain, and it has more to offer than a view of Split Rock. It is one of the few sites along or near the Parkway where you might find the late-summer-blooming smaller enchanter's nightshade. A plant of the cool north woods of Canada that ranges south to the high elevations of North Carolina, it is well worth looking for.

SPRING
Bluets
Wild Strawberry
Early Winter Cress
King Devil
Creeping Buttercup
Dwarf Cinquefoil
Great Laurel
Ox-eye Daisy
Blackberry
Mouse-ear Hawkweed
Pinxter-flower

SUMMER
Ox-eye Daisy
Common St. John's-
    wort

Evening Primrose
Whorled Loosestrife
Mouse-ear Chickweed
Yellow Wood Sorrel
Heal-all
Fringed Bindweed
Creeping Buttercup
Spiderwort
Deptford Pink
Queen Anne's Lace
King Devil
White-flowered Asters
Smaller Enchanter's
    Nightshade
Bull Thistle
Tall Bellflower
Greater Coreopsis

Daisy Fleabane
White Snakeroot

FALL
Heal-all
Queen Anne's Lace
Bull Thistle
White Snakeroot
Goldenrods
White-flowered Asters

Mile 306.6

*Grandfather Mountain View and
Parking Area* Elevation: 4,154'

This overlook offers an excellent view of 5,964-foot-high
Grandfather Mountain, the highest point on the Blue Ridge
Mountain range. This privately owned natural attraction features a mile-high, swinging footbridge, a nature museum, and
miles of alpine trails. Grandfather Mountain was known to the
Cherokee Indians as Tanawha, meaning "a fabulous hawk or
eagle."

An especially large crop of spring and summer wildflowers
grows here, including sweet cicely, dovesfoot cranesbill, and
starry campion.

SPRING
Hairy Bitter Cress
Common Blue Violet
Bluets
Henbit
Bird's-eye Speedwell
Common Winter Cress
Common Cinquefoil
Common Buttercup

Wild Strawberry
Kidneyleaf Buttercup
Blackberry
Mouse-ear Chickweed
Smooth Yellow Violet
English Plantain
Lily of the Valley
Sweet Cicely

SUMMER
Bluets
Wild Strawberry
Common Cinquefoil
Heal-all
Mountain Laurel
Blackberry
Common Buttercup
Hairy Hawkweed

Daisy Fleabane
Galax
Yarrow
Hop Clover
Common Speedwell
Ox-eye Daisy
Smooth Hawk's-beard
Dovesfoot Cranesbill
Great Laurel
Yellow Wood Sorrel

Pale Touch-me-not
Spotted Joe-pye-weed
Southern Harebell
Starry Campion
Sweet Joe-pye-weed
Goldenrods

FALL
Pale Touch-me-not
Yellow Wood Sorrel

Spotted Joe-pye-weed
Sweet Joe-pye-weed
Goldenrods
White Snakeroot
White-flowered Asters
Horse-Balm
Long-bristled
    Smartweed

Mile 308.2
❀ *Flat Rock Trail and Parking Area*

The parking area here provides access to the Flat Rock Trail, an easy, 30-minute, round-trip hike to Flat Rock, which affords an impressive view of Grandfather Mountain and the Linville Valley. Park Service exhibits along the trail describe native trees, plants, and animals.

Most of the wildflowers here, including the beautiful, springtime bluebead-lily, can be found along the trail. From mid- to late summer, look for the fly-poison's elongated white floral clusters near the trail's summit.

SPRING
Common Blue Violet
Dwarf Cinquefoil
Golden Alexander
Wood Anemone
Kidneyleaf Buttercup
Painted Trillium
Lily of the Valley
Halberd-leaved Violet
Jack-in-the-Pulpit
Dwarf Iris
Henbit
Mountain Bellwort
Bluebead-lily
Cleavers
False Lily of the Valley
Common Buttercup
Squaw-root
Hooked Buttercup
False Solomon's-seal

Common Fleabane
Blackberry
Sweet White Violet
Solomon's Seal

SUMMER
Common Buttercup
Common Cinquefoil
Heal-all
Large Houstonia
Solomon's Seal
Blackberry
Galax
Mountain Laurel
Hairy Hawkweed
Small's Ragwort
Trailing Arbutus
Common Milkweed
Water Hemlock
Great Laurel

Greater Coreopsis
Pale Touch-me-not
Spotted Touch-me-not
Wild Bergamot
Fly-Poison
Indian Pipe
Starry Campion

FALL
Spotted Touch-me-not
Pale Touch-me-not
Woodland Sunflower
Ox-eye
White Snakeroot
White-flowered Aster
Horse-Balm
Long-bristled
    Smartweed
Peruvian Daisy
Closed Gentian

Mile 316.5

✿ *Linville Falls Recreation Area*

This 440-acre recreation area features a visitor center, camp-grounds, restrooms, hiking, nature walks, trout fishing, and a picnic area. Viewing areas along the 1.4-mile spur road to the visitor center overlook the rushing waters of the Linville River.

A 1-mile trail from the visitor center to the base of the falls, with intermediate viewing platforms, is a gradual, up-and-down, easy trail bordered by many spring and summer wild-flowers. Wildflowers, especially fringed phacelia from mid- to late May, are also abundant at the River Bend Parking Area at Mile 0.4 of the spur road.

SPRING
Skunk Cabbage
Bluets
Henbit
Wild Strawberry
Common Blue Violet
Common Winter Cress
Kidneyleaf Buttercup
Flowering Dogwood
Common Buttercup
Giant Chickweed
Fringed Phacelia
Blackberry
Golden Ragwort
Bulbous Buttercup
Toothwort
Lily of the Valley
Painted Trillium
False Solomon's-seal

Mountain Laurel
May-apple

SUMMER
Common Buttercup
Heal-all
Mountain Laurel
Blackberry
Smooth Hawk's-beard
Hairy Hawkweed
Small's Ragwort
Daisy Fleabane
Galax
Creeping Buttercup
Ox-eye Daisy
Spiderwort
Yellow Wood Sorrel
Whorled Loosestrife
Great Laurel
Black-eyed Susan

Evening Primrose
Green-headed
  Coneflower
Mayweed
Virgin's Bower
Woolly Mullein
English Plantain
Deptford Pink
Maryland Golden
  Aster

FALL
Yellow Wood Sorrel
Heal-all
Virgin's Bower
Blue-flowered Asters
Goldenrods
White-flowered Asters
White Snakeroot

Mile 326

Heffner Gap Overlook Elevation: 3,067'

Long and straight, Linville Mountain dominates the view here. Closer and to the left, Honeycutt Mountain slopes gradually down into North Cove. Amanda Heffner, for whom this over-look is named, was a Civil War–era widow who raised a family on a nearby farm. No doubt Amanda had apple trees, because apples were a mainstay crop for many of the farmers in this region.

The trees are gone now, so we can only imagine the beauty of the springtime apple blossoms above the myriad of blooming wildflowers that still thrive here.

SPRING
Purple Dead Nettle
Hairy Bitter Cress
Common Winter Cress
Field Pansy
Wild Strawberry
Common Blue Violet
Yellow Wood Sorrel
Flowering Dogwood
Common Cinquefoil
Golden Ragwort
Dwarf Cinquefoil
Cleavers
Blackberry
White Campion
King Devil

SUMMER
Yellow Wood Sorrel
White Campion
Common Cinquefoil
Dwarf Cinquefoil
Golden Ragwort
Common Speedwell
English Plantain
Hop Clover
Cleavers
Yarrow
Queen Anne's Lace
Common Milkweed
Black-eyed Susan
Deptford Pink
Virgin's Bower

Flowering Spurge
Pale Touch-me-not
Horse-nettle
Goldenrods

FALL
Yellow Wood Sorrel
Tall Thistle
Virgin's Bower
Horse-nettle
Goldenrods
Pale Touch-me-not
Wing-stem

Mile 337.2

❀ *Deerlick Gap Overlook* Elevation: 3,452'

The view from this overlook is toward the south, with the long crest of Wood Mountain being the dominant feature. In the area around this overlook are several outcroppings of rock said to contain traces of saltpeter. Because salt is essential to deer's diet, they will travel great distances to lick the salt from the rocks. This gives rise to the name "Deerlick Gap."

This overlook offers one of the largest selections of spring wildflowers along the Parkway. Of special interest are the painted trillium and the spring vetch.

SPRING
Purple Dead Nettle
Dwarf Cinquefoil
Common Blue Violet
Wild Strawberry
Giant Chickweed

Gill-over-the-ground
Flowering Dogwood
Common Winter Cress
Common Cinquefoil
Field Pansy
Golden Ragwort

Golden Alexander
Painted Trillium
Blackberry
King Devil
Crested Dwarf Iris
Mouse-ear Chickweed

Mountain Bellwort	Horse-nettle	Virgin's Bower
Spring Vetch	Spiderwort	White Snakeroot
Solomon's Seal	Spreading Dogbane	
Spiderwort	Heart-leaved Skullcap	
	Hoary Mountain Mint	FALL
SUMMER	Flowering Spurge	Horse-nettle
Yellow Wood Sorrel	Greater Coreopsis	Virgin's Bower
Solomon's Seal	Ox-eye Daisy	Goldenrods
Bowman's-root	Hop Clover	White Snakeroot
Thimbleweed	Pigeonberry	Blue-flowered Asters
Yarrow	Common Milkweed	Tall Thistle
Daisy Fleabane	Evening Primrose	Silverrod
Lesser Stitchwort	Spotted Joe-pye-weed	

Mile 339.5
❀ Crabtree Meadows Recreation Area

This recreation area features a coffee shop, gift shop, hiking trail, campground, and service station. A short trail from the parking area leads to an outdoor amphitheater, where periodic summer-evening programs cover a variety of topics related to nature and mountain living.

Look for wildflowers along the trail and in the open fields around the amphitheater. Also be sure to check the wooded island in front of the coffee shop. This is where you will find springtime pink lady's slippers. Summer brings the Indian pipes, while asters and thistles dominate the fall landscape.

SPRING	Lyre-leaved Sage	Hairy Hawkweed
Bluets	Common Fleabane	Daisy Fleabane
Common Blue Violet	Large-flowered	Yarrow
Common Winter Cress	Trillium	Great Laurel
Wild Strawberry	Hispid Buttercup	Common Milkweed
Field Pansy	Pink Lady's Slipper	Flowering Spurge
Dwarf Cinquefoil	False Solomon's-seal	Black-eyed Susan
Giant Chickweed	Showy Orchis	Thimbleweed
Common Cinquefoil	May-apple	Wild Blue Phlox
Golden Ragwort		Ox-eye Daisy
Flowering Dogwood	SUMMER	Butterfly-weed
Golden Alexander	King Devil	Evening Primrose
Common Buttercup	Blackberry	Pale Indian-plantain
Crested Dwarf Iris	Solomon's Seal	Wild Bergamot
King Devil	Large Houstonia	Rough Avens

Horse-nettle
Gray Beard-tongue
Spreading Dogbane
Heal-all
Indian Pipe
Goldenrods
Sweet Joe-pye-weed
White Snakeroot

FALL
Sweet Joe-pye-weed
Horse-nettle
Heal-all
Goldenrods
White-flowered Asters
Pale Indian-plantain
Tall Thistle

Blue-flowered Asters
White Snakeroot
Silverrod

Mile 350.4

Green Knob Overlook Elevation: 4,761'

Green Knob, directly behind this overlook, reaches up to an elevation of 4,950 feet. The view from here looks out over the headwaters of the Catawba River in an area the Catawba Indians once called home.

One of my favorite wildflowers, thimbleweed (also called tall anemone), is a midsummer bloomer here.

SPRING
Bluets
Wild Strawberry
Common Blue Violet
Common Winter
    Cress
Giant Chickweed
Bird's-eye Speedwell
Common Cinquefoil
Golden Ragwort
Blackberry
Mouse-ear
    Chickweed
White Campion
King Devil
Yarrow

SUMMER
White Campion
Common Cinquefoil
Mountain Laurel
Yarrow
Ox-eye Daisy
Hairy Hawkweed
Daisy Fleabane
Spiderwort
Hop Clover
Dovesfoot Cranesbill
Thimbleweed
Deptford Pink
Rough-fruited
    Cinquefoil
Hedge-nettle
Yellow Wood Sorrel

Whorled Loosestrife
Poke Milkweed
White Sweet Clover
Evening Primrose
Southern Harebell
Woodland Sunflower
White-flowered Asters
Goldenrods

FALL
Woodland Sunflower
Yellow Wood Sorrel
Goldenrods
Hedge Bindweed
White-flowered Asters
Ox-eye

Mile 359.9

✿ Balsam Gap Overlook Elevation: 5,317'

Balsam Gap marks the juncture between the Black Mountains to the north and the Great Craggies to the south. The forest surrounding the overlook is reminiscent of the forests of Canada, consisting mostly of red spruce and Fraser fir.

Across the Parkway from the overlook is the trailhead to the Mountains to Sea Trail, which disappears into the forest along the track bed of an old logging railroad. Around the entrance to this trail is an excellent spot to look for spring wildflowers, especially the trilliums, wood anemone, and the Carolina spring-beauty. Look carefully and you might find the Dutchman's-breeches. Late summer and fall brings forth the beautiful filmy angelica, the colorful asters, and the stately Joe-pye-weeds.

SPRING	False Solomon's-seal	Spotted Joe-pye-weed
Bluets	May-apple	Wild Bergamot
Common Blue Violet		Filmy Angelica
Giant Chickweed		White Snakeroot
Red Trillium	SUMMER	
Wild Strawberry	Blackberry	
Painted Trillium	Dwarf Cinquefoil	FALL
Wood Anemone	Common Cinquefoil	Pale Touch-me-not
Dwarf Cinquefoil	Heal-all	Spotted Joe-pye-weed
Kidneyleaf Buttercup	Blue-eyed Grass	Heal-all
Nodding Trillium	Daisy Fleabane	Filmy Angelica
Golden Ragwort	Green-headed	White-flowered Asters
Dutchman's-breeches	Coneflower	Blue-flowered Asters
Carolina Spring-beauty	Hairy Hawkweed	White Snakeroot
	Yarrow	

Mile 364.5

Craggy Dome View Elevation: 5,220'

This overlook is part of the Craggy Gardens Recreation Area. Nearby, at about Mile 364.6, is a visitor center with exhibits, an information desk, and self-guided tours. A spur road at Mile 367.6 has comfort stations and provides access to hiking trails.

This expansive, two-tiered overlook provides an excellent view of Craggy Dome and hosts a good selection of summer wildflowers.

SPRING	Common Blue Violet	Common Buttercup
Bluets	Carolina Spring-beauty	Blackberry
Strawberry	Golden Ragwort	Common Cinquefoil

SUMMER
Bluets
Common Buttercup
Giant Chickweed
Blackberry
Common Cinquefoil
King Devil
Lesser Stitchwort
Great Laurel
Yarrow
Smooth Hawk's-beard
Ox-eye Daisy
Common St. John's-
    wort

Hedge Bindweed
Pale Touch-me-not
Wild Bergamot
Bee-balm
Wild Blue Phlox
Black Cohosh
Spotted Joe-pye-weed
Filmy Angelica
White Snakeroot
White-flowered Asters
Bush Honeysuckle
Whorled Loosestrife

FALL
Heal-all
Hedge Bindweed
Filmy Angelica
Whorled Loosestrife
Yarrow
Spotted Joe-pye-weed
Goldenrods
White-flowered Asters
White Snakeroot

Mile 373.9

Bull Creek Valley View Elevation: 3,483'

Bull Creek Valley, directly below, cradles Bull Creek as it flows southward to join the Swannanoa River. In the distance, across the valley, are the Swannanoa Mountains. Buffalo roamed this region centuries ago, and the last one, a giant bull buffalo, was killed on this spot in 1799 by a settler named Joseph Rice. The killing of the bull buffalo might have led to the naming of Bull Creek and Bull Creek Valley.

One of the prettiest of spring wildflowers, the small-flowered phacelia, grows here. Look for it along the edges of the wooded areas around the overlook.

SPRING
Wild Strawberry
Yellow Wood Sorrel
Hooked Buttercup
Wild Geranium
Blackberry
Small-flowered Phacelia
Lyre-leaved Sage
Flowering Dogwood
Nodding Trillium
Early Meadow Rue
Solomon's Seal

SUMMER
Blackberry
Early Meadow Rue
Daisy Fleabane
King Devil
Ox-eye Daisy
Yarrow
Yellow Wood Sorrel
Asiatic Dayflower
Tufted Vetch
Horse-nettle
Spiderwort

Hedge Bindweed
English Plantain
Evening Primrose
Pale Touch-me-not
Peruvian Daisy
Poke Milkweed
Gray Beard-tongue
Spotted Joe-pye-weed
Woodland Sunflower
Tall Thistle

FALL
Pale Touch-me-not
Spotted Joe-pye-weed

Woodland Sunflower
Tall Thistle
Flowering Spurge

White-flowered Asters
Goldenrods

Mile 380

Haw Creek Valley View Elevation: 2,720'

This view, facing west, looks out over Haw Creek. Beyond the creek and to the left is Cisco Mountain. At night the lights of Asheville, North Carolina, illuminate the skyline.

Carolina cranesbill blooms here in the springtime, and if you take a close look at the seedpods, you'll know why it is called "cranesbill."

SPRING
Wild Strawberry
Henbit
Bird's-eye Speedwell
Common Cinquefoil
Yellow Wood Sorrel
Lyre-leaved Sage
Blackberry
Tufted Vetch
King Devil
Flowering Spurge
Carolina Cranesbill
Small-flowered Phacelia
Spring Vetch

Cat's-ear
Cleavers

SUMMER
Yellow Wood Sorrel
Cat's-ear
Yarrow
Spiderwort
Balsam Ragwort
Daisy Fleabane
Flowering Spurge
Hedge Bindweed
Greater Coreopsis
Woolly Mullein

English Plantain
Common St. John's-
wort
Smooth Hawk's-beard
Hoary Mountain Mint
Evening Primrose

FALL
Flowering Spurge
Southern Harebell
Goldenrods
Hyssop-leaved Boneset
White-flowered Asters
Blue-flowered Asters

Mile 399.7

Bad Fork Valley Overlook Elevation: 3,350'

This overlook is perched on the edge of Bad Fork Valley, from which the Pisgah Ledge is visible on the distant horizon. The highest point of the ledge is Mount Pisgah. Also in the distance, but closer to the overlook, Avery Creek Road cuts its way along the side of Fannie Ridge.

Springtime common fleabane and summertime daisy fleabane grow profusely around this overlook.

Wild Strawberry
Common Cinquefoil
Hop Clover
Mouse-ear Chickweed
Yellow Wood Sorrel
Blackberry
King Devil
Small's Ragwort
Carolina Cranesbill
Common Fleabane
English Plantain
Tufted Vetch
Mountain Laurel
Early Meadow Rue
Yarrow

SUMMER
Yarrow
Yellow Wood Sorrel
Tufted Vetch
King Devil
Smooth Hawk's-beard
Hop Clover
Daisy Fleabane
Ox-eye Daisy
Deptford Pink
Large Houstonia
White Campion
Greater Coreopsis
Horse-nettle
English Plantain
Queen Anne's Lace

Woolly Mullein
Goldenrods

FALL
White-flowered Asters
Horse-nettle
Hoary Tick-trefoil
Goldenrods
White Snakeroot
Wing-stem
Slender Bush-Clover

Mile 403.8

Big Ridge Overlook Elevation: 3,820'

This overlook faces southeast with the roller-coaster profile of Big Ridge in the distance. Beartree Ridge is close-by, jutting out from the Parkway on the right. Directly across the Parkway is a path to the Shut-in Trail, which leads in one direction to Stony Bald and in the other to Bent Creek.

The embankment behind this overlook hosts a healthy colony of the yellowish, leafless squaw-root, a strange-looking plant indeed.

SPRING
Common Blue Violet
Common Cinquefoil
Common Winter Cress
Kidneyleaf Buttercup
Mouse-ear Chickweed
Blackberry
King Devil
Squaw-root
Yellow Wood Sorrel
Common Fleabane
Mountain Bellwort

False Solomon's-seal
Solomon's Seal

SUMMER
Solomon's Seal
Yarrow
Smooth Hawk's-beard
Daisy Fleabane
Ox-eye Daisy
Spiderwort
Common Milkweed
Large Houstonia
Whorled Loosestrife

Greater Coreopsis
English Plantain
Queen Anne's Lace
Daisy Fleabane
Yellow Wood Sorrel
Pigeonberry
Wild Blue Phlox
Wing-stem
Hollow Joe-pye-weed
Virgin's Bower
Evening Primrose
Heal-all

FALL		
Queen Anne's Lace	Heal-all	Wing-stem
Virgin's Bower	Pale Indian-plantain	White Snakeroot
	Goldenrods	

Mile 409.4

Funneltop View Elevation: 4,925'

This dip in the ridgeline, known as Frying Pan Gap, lies in the shadow of Frying Pan Mountain, a short distance to the west. Funneltop Mountain, which looks something like an inverted funnel, is in view to the southeast. Early hunters, herdsmen, and travelers found the gap to be a perfect campsite because of protection from the wind and the presence of spring water nearby. It is believed that a large iron skillet was left here at the campsite for the use of any camper who happened along. Thus the name, Frying Pan Gap.

Silverrod, the only white member of the goldenrod family, blooms here in the late summer and early fall.

SPRING	SUMMER	
Bluets	Mountain Laurel	Deptford Pink
Common Cinquefoil	Smooth Hawk's-beard	Whorled Loosestrife
Wild Strawberry	Hop Clover	Heal-all
Common Blue Violet	Golden Ragwort	White Snakeroot
Golden Ragwort	Evening Primrose	English Plantain
Hop Clover	Mouse-ear Hawkweed	Goldenrods
Dwarf Cinquefoil	Gray Beard-tongue	
Mouse-ear Hawkweed	Yarrow	FALL
...ll's Ragwort	Large Houstonia	Yellow Wood Sorrel
... Fleabane	Common Speedwell	Heal-all
...k's-beard	Flowering Spurge	Whorled Loosestrife
	Black-eyed Susan	Goldenrods
	Great Laurel	Silverrod
	...e-eye Daisy	White-flowered Asters
	... Fleabane	White Snakeroot

of forests
who

approaches to forestry. Pinchot's forestry methods included erosion control, tree planting, and conservation. This was in direct contrast to the uncontrolled logging that in early times scarred much of Appalachia. Pinchot laid the groundwork for the modern forestry methods used today. Not far away, near the city of Brevard, North Carolina, is the Cradle of Forestry Museum. It can be reached via Route 276, the old Wagon Gap Road, which crosses the Parkway at Mile 411.9.

Spring and summer wildflowers are abundant here. Look especially for the springtime mouse-ear hawkweed and notice its small, roundish, hairy leaves—they really do look like mouse ears.

SPRING

Wild Strawberry
Common Blue Violet
Common Cinquefoil
Common Winter Cress
Golden Ragwort
Mouse-ear Chickweed
Small's Ragwort
Hop Clover
Blackberry
King Devil
Mouse-ear Hawkweed
Plantain-leaved
    Pussytoes
Mountain Laurel

SUMMER

Mountain Laurel
Golden Ragwort

Mouse-ear Hawkweed
Hairy Hawkweed
Smooth Hawk's-beard
Large Houstonia
Yarrow
Ox-eye Daisy
Balsam Ragwort
Whorled Loosestrife
Hop Clover
Gray Beard-tongue
Heal-all
Hoary Mountain
    Mint
Evening Primrose
Daisy Fleabane
Deptford Pink
Sundrops
Great Coreopsis
Wild Blue Phlox

Pale Touch-me-not
Woolly Mullein
Ox-eye
Goldenrods

FALL

Goldenrods
Ox-eye
Wild Blue Phlox
Heal-all
Slender Bush-Clover
Silverrod
White Snakeroot
White-flowered Asters
Blue-flowered Asters

Mile 417

Looking Glass Rock View El

The massive, 400-foot-hi
Rock face this overlo
apparent in wint
the rock fre
of ice
f

A large, late-spring crop of common lousewort, also known as wood betony, can be found among the rocks on the steep slope behind this overlook.

SPRING
Bluets
Common Cinquefoil
Wild Strawberry
Common Blue Violet
Mouse-ear Chickweed
Golden Ragwort
King Devil
Common Fleabane
Lyre-leaved Sage
Pinxter-flower
Mountain Bellwort
Common Lousewort

SUMMER
Daisy Fleabane
Hairy Hawkweed
Mouse-ear Hawkweed
Mountain Laurel
Asiatic Dayflower
Yarrow
Shrubby St. John's-wort
Large Houstonia
Common Milkweed
Smooth Hawk's-beard
Heal-all
Sundrops
Pigeonberry

Hedge-nettle
Wild Bergamot
Spotted Joe-pye-weed
Ox-eye
Goldenrods

FALL
Spotted Joe-pye-weed
Ox-eye
Heal-all
Goldenrods
White-flowered Asters
White Snakeroot
Blue-flowered Asters

Mile 421.7

Fetterbush Overlook Elevation: 5,494'

Fetterbush, along with several other members of the heath family (such as mountain laurel and great laurel), can be found growing in the surrounding area. To identify this spring-blooming shrub of the high-country balds, look for its 1- to 2-inch-long evergreen leaves and terminal clusters of small, white, urn-shaped flowers.

SPRING
Bluets
Common Blue Violet
Common Cinquefoil
Common Winter Cress
Wild Strawberry
Golden Ragwort
Common Fleabane
Sweet White Violet
Smooth Rock-cress
Pinxter-flower
Mountain Laurel

SUMMER
Bluets
Hairy Hawkweed
Sundrops
Daisy Fleabane
Mouse-ear Hawkweed
Ox-eye Daisy
Yarrow
Shrubby St. John's-wort
Bush Honeysuckle
Heal-all

Green-headed
   Coneflower
White Snakeroot
Goldenrods

FALL
Heal-all
Goldenrods
White-flowered Asters
Blue-flowered Asters
White Snakeroot

Mile 427.5

Bear Pen Gap Parking Area Elevation: 5,560'

Bears will wander a considerable distance in search of food and often used gaps such as this one in crossing mountain ridges. Early-twentieth-century hunters, knowing of the bear's travel habits, built their bear-pen traps in these gaps. Piney Mountain Creek originates below this overlook and runs through the valley between Piney Mountain and Sugar Creek Ridge.

Hoary mountain mint grows here in abundance. If you are here in midsummer, you might be able to find it by closing your eyes and following the pungent, minty odor.

SPRING
Bluets
Wild Strawberry
Common Blue Violet
Mouse-ear Chickweed
Wood Anemone
Golden Ragwort
Dutchman's-breeches
Carolina Spring-beauty
Sweet White Clover
Mouse-ear Hawkweed

SUMMER
Hairy Hawkweed
Mouse-ear Hawkweed

Blackberry
Yellow Wood Sorrel
Tall Buttercup
Common Cinquefoil
Yarrow
Early Meadow Rue
Hoary Mountain Mint
Pale Touch-me-not
*Common St. John's-
    wort*
Ox-eye Daisy
Hedge-nettle
Heal-all
Hedge Bindweed
Bush Honeysuckle

*Green-headed
    Coneflower*
White-flowered Asters
White Snakeroot

FALL
Pale Touch-me-not
Yellow Wood Sorrel
Hedge Bindweed
*Green-headed
    Coneflower*
White-flowered Asters
Heal-all
White Snakeroot

Mile 430.6

Beartail Ridge Parking Area Elevation: 5,872'

Actually, two ridges converge here: Big Beartail Ridge, on the left, runs to the northeast, and Little Beartail Ridge, on the right, runs due east. Bears were abundant here at one time, and many of the area's ridges, knobs, and creeks were named with the bears in mind. One of the region's greatest bear hunters, a fellow named Israel Medford, lived a short distance from here at the foot of Licklog Mountain.

One of the most spectacular of the late summer wildflowers, the green-headed coneflower, can be found blooming here. It grows to a height of 12 feet and has blossoms with reflexed, golden petals surrounding a green, pincushion-like disk.

SPRING
Bluets
Wild Strawberry
Common Blue Violet
Common Cinquefoil
Mouse-ear Chickweed
Field Pansy
Golden Ragwort
Blackberry
Carolina Spring-beauty
Pinxter-flower
Sweet White Violet

SUMMER
Bluets
Blackberry
Common Cinquefoil
Mouse-ear Hawkweed
Hairy Hawkweed
Common Speedwell
Yarrow
Lesser Stitchwort
Common Buttercup
Green-headed
    Coneflower
Heal-all
Hedge Bindweed

Southern Harebell
Filmy Angelica
Wild Bergamot
White-flowered Asters
White Snakeroot

FALL
Filmy Angelica
Heal-all
Yellow Wood Sorrel
White-flowered Asters
White Snakeroot
Goldenrods
Blue-flowered Asters

Mile 432.7

Lone Bald Overlook Elevation: 5,635'

Lone Bald, on the near right, is not as bald as it used to be. Today it is covered with a growth of young deciduous trees and an ever increasing crop of red spruce. At one time, however, a lone spruce tree (a balsam) dominated the top of the mountain and was known as the Lone Balsam. Then one day the tree was toppled in the wake of a strong storm, and the mountain became Lone Bald.

The springtime star of this site is the cut-leaved toothwort. Look for its cluster of pinkish flowers and whorls of three leaves, each divided into three narrow segments.

SPRING
Bluets
Wild Strawberry
Bird's-eye Speedwell
Common Blue Violet
Common Winter Cress
Common Cinquefoil
Cut-leaved Toothwort
Golden Ragwort
Common Fleabane

SUMMER
Golden Ragwort
Common Fleabane
Yarrow
Hairy Hawkweed
Common Buttercup
Cow Parsnip
Hop Clover
Mouse-ear Hawkweed
Common Speedwell

Ox-eye Daisy
Daisy Fleabane
Evening Primrose
Hedge-nettle
Wild Blue Phlox
Wild Bergamot
Hoary Mountain
    Mint
Heal-all
Hedge Bindweed

Green-headed	FALL	White Snakeroot
Coneflower	Heal-all	Blue-flowered Asters
Bush Honeysuckle	Hedge Bindweed	White-flowered Asters
White-flowered Asters	Green-headed	Goldenrods
	Coneflower	Silverrod

Mile 435.2

Doubletop Mountain Overlook Elevation: 5,365'

This overlook is perched on top of Flat Gap and offers an excellent view of Doubletop Mountain. Its double humps can be seen just to the right of center of the overlook. A little farther to the right and a little closer is Dark Ridge, extending out from the Parkway.

If you want to see cow parsnip, this is the place to stop. The overlook has the best midsummer crop on the Parkway. It is a tall plant, up to 10 feet high, with rounded clusters of tiny flowers and maple-like leaves.

SPRING	Hairy Hawkweed	Green-headed
Wild Strawberry	Yarrow	Coneflower
Common Blue Violet	Large Houstonia	Hedge Bindweed
Wood Anemone	Mouse-ear Hawkweed	Yellow Wood Sorrel
Mouse-ear Chickweed	Ox-eye Daisy	White Snakeroot
Bluets	Spiderwort	
Golden Ragwort	Common Speedwell	FALL
Giant Chickweed	Mountain Laurel	Hedge Bindweed
Wild Geranium	Sundrops	Green-headed
May-apple	Cow Parsnip	Coneflower
Smooth Rock-cress	Daisy Fleabane	Yellow Wood Sorrel
	Wild Bergamot	White Snakeroot
SUMMER	Evening Primrose	Blue-flowered Asters
Blackberry	Wild Blue Phlox	Goldenrods
Wild Geranium		

Mile 438.9

Steestachee Bald View Elevation: 4,780'

Steestachee Bald, on the ridge line to the right, rolls up to an elevation of 5,690 feet. North of here the Parkway loops around and cuts across Steestachee Bald's middle. The word "Steestachee" comes from the Cherokee Indian term *Tsi-ste-tsi*, meaning "mouse" or "rat." Although deer mice are common in the area, no one knows for sure why the bald is called "Steestachee."

Springtime may-apples are plentiful in the woods around this overlook. Look for the white, waxy flower dangling beneath two large umbrella-like leaves.

SPRING
Common Buttercup
Wild Strawberry
Common Winter Cress
Golden Ragwort
Small's Ragwort
Blackberry
Lyre-leaved Sage
King Devil
May-apple

SUMMER
Blackberry
Mountain Laurel
Ox-eye Daisy

Deptford Pink
Whorled Loosestrife
Mouse-ear Hawkweed
Yarrow
Hop Clover
Wild Geranium
Lesser Stitchwort
Hairy Hawkweed
Smooth Hawk's-beard
Daisy Fleabane
Purple-flowering
  Raspberry
Flowering Spurge
Greater Coreopsis
Evening Primrose

Common St. John's-
  wort
Pale Indian-plantain
Queen Anne's Lace
Virgin's Bower
White Snakeroot

FALL
Virgin's Bower
Evening Primrose
Heal-all
White-flowered Asters
Blue-flowered Asters
Goldenrods
White Snakeroot

Mile 440.8
❀ *Waynesville View* Elevation: 4,110'

The town of Waynesville, settled in about 1800, spreads out in the valley below. It is the seat of Haywood County, and its Main Street is a mecca for antique collectors and shoppers. Waynesville was named for the Revolutionary War general "Mad Anthony" Wayne, so known because of his reckless courage.

In the springtime, look for the large-flowered trillium and the early meadow rue that bloom here.

SPRING
Common Blue Violet
Mouse-ear Chickweed
Wild Strawberry
Common Buttercup
Golden Ragwort
Flowering Dogwood
Blackberry

Lyre-leaved Sage
Long-leaved Bluets
Large-flowered
  Trillium
May-apple
Early Meadow Rue

SUMMER
Hop Clover
Yellow Wood Sorrel
Common Buttercup
Cow Parsnip
Purple-flowering
  Raspberry
Yarrow

Daisy Fleabane
Heal-all
Spiderwort
Spotted Joe-pye-weed
Tall Bellflower
Evening Primrose
Pale Touch-me-not
Wild Bergamot

Ox-eye
Virgin's Bower
Blue-flowered Asters
White Snakeroot

FALL
Heal-all
Yellow Wood Sorrel

Sweet Joe-pye-weed
White Snakeroot
Pale Touch-me-not
White-flowered Asters
Blue-flowered Asters
Goldenrods

Mile 444.5

Orchards Overlook Elevation: 3,810'

This loop-drive overlook is named for the many apple orchards that grow along Richland Creek in the valley below.
Route 23 parallels the creek and is visible as it runs from Balsam Gap to the town of Waynesville.

This overlook features a spectacular early fall concentration
of pale touch-me-not.

SPRING
Common Blue Violet
Wild Strawberry
Common Winter Cress
Giant Chickweed
Common Cinquefoil
Mouse-ear Hawkweed
Wild Geranium
Blackberry
May-apple

SUMMER
Heal-all
Yellow Wood Sorrel
Mouse-ear Hawkweed

Hop Clover
Hairy Hawkweed
Large Houstonia
Horse-nettle
Cat's-ear
Ox-eye Daisy
Lesser Stitchwort
Spiderwort
Daisy Fleabane
Common Milkweed
White Campion
Wild Bergamot
Pale Touch-me-not
Black Cohosh
Queen Anne's Lace

Black-eyed Susan
Pale Indian-plantain
Virgin's Bower
Asiatic Dayflower

FALL
Virgin's Bower
Yellow Wood Sorrel
Black-eyed Susan
Pale Touch-me-not
Woodland Sunflower
Heal-all
White Snakeroot

Mile 446

Woodfin Valley View Elevation: 4,120'

Woodfin Creek cascades down the side of Mount Lyn Lowry
and rushes through the Woodfin Valley below. The creek can-
not be seen, but the sound of the running waters, which can be
heard from this overlook, is invigorating yet restful, a welcome

accompaniment to a search for the bright violet blossoms of the spiderworts that grow around the edges of this overlook.

SPRING
Bluets
Common Blue Violet
Wild Strawberry
Giant Chickweed
Common Cinquefoil
Common Buttercup
Golden Ragwort
Hooked Buttercup
Mouse-ear Hawkweed
King Devil
Blackberry
Common Fleabane
Mountain Bellwort
Lyre-leaved Sage

SUMMER
Mouse-ear Hawkweed
Hairy Hawkweed
Daisy Fleabane
Spiderwort
Mountain Laurel
Black-eyed Susan
Cat's-ear
Large Houstonia
Ox-eye Daisy
Yarrow
Flowering Spurge
Smooth Hawk's-beard
English Plantain
Hop Clover

Heal-all
Greater Coreopsis
Evening Primrose
Pale Indian-plantain
Woodland Sunflower
Goldenrods

FALL
Yellow Wood Sorrel
Woodland Sunflower
Heal-all
White Snakeroot
White-flowered Asters
Blue-flowered Asters
Goldenrods

Mile 448.1

Wesner Bald View Elevation: 4,914'

Due east of this overlook, across Scott Creek Valley, Wesner Bald rises to an elevation of 5,560 feet. A section of Route 23 can be seen running through the valley on its way to the town of Waynesville.

The embankment near this overlook hosts a colony of perfoliate bellwort. Look for the dangling, yellowish green flowers from mid- to late May.

SPRING
Bluets
Wild Strawberry
Common Blue Violet
Common Winter
   Cress
Giant Chickweed
Golden Ragwort
Common Cinquefoil
Common Fleabane
Mouse-ear Hawkweed
Hispid Buttercup
Perfoliate Bellwort

Early Meadow Rue
Solomon's Seal
Common Lousewort

SUMMER
Solomon's Seal
Smooth Hawk's-beard
Yellow Wood Sorrel
Common Speedwell
Mouse-ear Hawkweed
Hop Clover
Blackberry
Large Houstonia

Bowman's-root
Spiderwort
Water Hemlock
Deptford Pink
Daisy Fleabane
Mountain Laurel
Yarrow
Black-eyed Susan
Greater Coreopsis
Wild Bergamot
Pale Indian-plantain
Poke Milkweed
Heal-all

Woodland Sunflower
White Snakeroot
Goldenrods

FALL
Yellow Wood Sorrel
Heal-all
Woodland Sunflower
Pale Indian-plantain

White Snakeroot
White-flowered Asters
Blue-flowered Asters
Goldenrods

Mile 451.2

Waterrock Knob Overlook and Trail Elevation: 5,820'

This unusual, loop-drive overlook has three viewpoints, two facing due east, letting one scan the ridges of the southern Appalachians, and one facing due west, affording a view of the Great Balsam Ridge as it stretches out toward the Great Smokies. A partially paved trail leads to the top of Waterrock Knob, where you find yourself amid a ghostly colony of long-dead Fraser firs. The air is cool and fresh, and you can nearly reach up and touch the sky.

A special treat at the overlook is the small patch of late fall wintergreen. Its thick, shiny, oval leaves and tiny white, waxy, bell-shaped flowers can be found along the edge of the walkway leading to the shelter and restrooms.

SPRING
Bluets
Wild Strawberry
Dwarf Cinquefoil
Common Blue Violet
Pinxter-flower
Common Winter Cress

SUMMER
Hop Clover
Common Cinquefoil
Mouse-ear Hawkweed

Hairy Hawkweed
Smooth Hawk's-beard
Lesser Stitchwort
Blackberry
Great Laurel
Yarrow
Bluets
Dwarf Cinquefoil
Ox-eye Daisy
Heal-all
Black-eyed Susan
Evening Primrose

Bush Honeysuckle
White-flowered Asters
Goldenrods

FALL
Goldenrods
Heal-all
White-flowered Asters
Yellow Wood Sorrel
Closed Gentian
Wintergreen

Mile 453.4

Hornbuckle Valley View Elevation: 5,105'

The headwaters of Hornbuckle Creek form along the slopes below this overlook then drop into Hornbuckle Valley and rush on to join Soco Creek in the Soco Valley. The Plott Balsam Range is visible in the distance to the left.

When summer flowers are blooming here, they present a rainbow of colors. You will see the white of the ox-eye daisy, the orange of the flame azalea, the yellow of the evening primrose, the pink of the hollow Joe-pye-weed, and the blue of the blue-flowered asters.

SPRING
Bluets
Dwarf Cinquefoil
Wild Strawberry
Wood Anemone
Mouse-ear Chickweed
Blackberry
Common Buttercup
Mouse-ear Hawkweed
Large-flowered
   Trillium

SUMMER
Bluets
Common Cinquefoil

Mouse-ear Hawkweed
Large Houstonia
Dwarf Cinquefoil
Hop Clover
Mountain Laurel
Ox-eye Daisy
Hairy Hawkweed
Smooth Hawk's-beard
Flame Azalea
Daisy Fleabane
Large Houstonia
Evening Primrose
Goldenrods
Black-eyed Susan
Hollow Joe-pye-weed

Woodland Sunflower
White Snakeroot
Blue-flowered Asters

FALL
Heal-all
Woodland Sunflower
Black-eyed Susan
Goldenrods
White Snakeroot
Blue-flowered Asters
White-flowered Asters

Mile 457.9

Plott Balsams View Elevation: 5,020'

The massive Plott Balsam Range rises up directly across the valley. The name commemorates Henry Plott, the son of a German immigrant who lived on these mountain slopes in the early 1800s. Henry Plott was best known for his skills at raising and breeding the finest bear-hunting dogs in the region. He and his descendants developed a line of dogs known as Plott Bear Hounds. Even today, the breed are considered prize hunting dogs.

Wild oats, a plant belonging to the bellwort family, is found only near the southern end of the Parkway, and a colony grows here. See if you can find them from mid- to late spring. They are similar to mountain bellwort but grow in colonies.

SPRING
Shepherd's-purse
Common Winter Cress

Wild Strawberry
Golden Ragwort
Common Cinquefoil

Common Fleabane
Common Lousewort
Wild Oats

SUMMER
Yellow Wood Sorrel
Golden Ragwort
Common Cinquefoil
Daisy Fleabane
Mountain Laurel
Dwarf Cinquefoil
Lesser Stitchwort
Spiderwort
Gray Beard-tongue
Large Houstonia

Bowman's-root
Ox-eye Daisy
Yarrow
Common Lousewort
Pigeonberry
White Sweet Clover
Greater Coreopsis
Evening Primrose
Starry Campion
Southern Harebell

Woodland Sunflower
White Snakeroot

FALL
Yellow Wood Sorrel
Woodland Sunflower
Pigeonberry
White Snakeroot
Goldenrods
White-flowered Asters

Mile 458.9

❀ *Lickstone Ridge Overlook* Elevation: 5,150'

Generations of farmers along this flat-top ridge covered flat stones with salt in areas where their cattle grazed. The "lickstones" provided a steady supply of salt needed by the animals for their diet. The valley below Lickstone Ridge is the site of an Indian reservation that was home to the great Cherokee tribe that once ruled this region.

The elegant, midsummer Turk's-cap lily grows at the base of the embankment behind this overlook. Look for the blossom's bright orange, dark-spotted, reflexed petals surrounding protruding filament-like stamens.

SPRING
Common Cinquefoil
Wild Strawberry
Common Winter Cress
Common Blue Violet
Golden Ragwort
Mouse-ear Chickweed
Sweet White Violet
Kidneyleaf Buttercup
Smooth Rock-cress
Wild Geranium
Squaw-root
False Solomon's-seal
Common Lousewort

SUMMER
Ox-eye Daisy
Common Cinquefoil

Blackberry
Hairy Hawkweed
Yarrow
Wild Geranium
Solomon's Seal
Mountain Laurel
Evening Primrose
Bowman's-root
Yellow Goat's-beard
Daisy Fleabane
Spiderwort
Smooth Hawk's-beard
Heal-all
Sundrops
Pale Touch-me-not
Common St. John's-wort
Poke Milkweed

Sweet Joe-pye-weed
Green-headed
    Coneflower
Turk's-cap Lily
Yellow Wood Sorrel
Hollow Joe-pye-weed
Filmy Angelica
White Snakeroot

FALL
Hollow Joe-pye-weed
Filmy Angelica
White Snakeroot
Pale Touch-me-not
Yellow Wood Sorrel
Blue-flowered Asters
White-flowered Asters
Great Lobelia

Mile 460.8

Jenkins Ridge Overlook Elevation: 4,445'

Jonas Jenkins, an early settler in this area, lived on the ridge that now carries his name. A creek on the far side of the ridge was also named in his memory.

Stop here in the late summer and fall and look for the pale touch-me-not. Its pale yellow, sac-like blossoms hang like pendant jewels among bright green leaves. The ripened seedpods pop open when touched.

SPRING
Common Cinquefoil
Wild Strawberry
Common Winter Cress
Common Blue Violet
Golden Ragwort
Cleavers
Mouse-ear Hawkweed
Lyre-leaved Sage

SUMMER
Daisy Fleabane
Hop Clover
Cat's-ear
Common Cinquefoil

Ox-eye Daisy
Spiderwort
Yarrow
Sundrops
Lesser Stitchwort
Smooth Hawk's-beard
Yellow Wood Sorrel
Heal-all
Wild Blue Phlox
Evening Primrose
Pale Touch-me-not
Tall Bellflower
Turk's-cap Lily
Green-headed
    Coneflower

Woodland Sunflower
Ox-eye
Virgin's Bower

FALL
Yellow Wood Sorrel
Ox-eye
Virgin's Bower
Woodland Sunflower
White Snakeroot
Blue-flowered Asters
Pale Touch-me-not
Hollow Joe-pye-weed

Mile 467.8

Raven Fork View Elevation: 2,400'

In the valley 300 feet below this overlook, a fork of Raven Creek is visible as it parallels Big Cove Road. Across the valley, Thomas Ridge rises up in the distance.

A number of plants with yellow, dandelion-like flowers grow here. See if you can find the springtime King Devil and mouse-ear hawkweed and the summertime smooth hawk's-beard and cat's-ear.

SPRING
Bluets
Common Blue Violet
Wild Strawberry

Field Pansy
Flowering Dogwood
Yellow Wood Sorrel
Lyre-leaved Sage

Carolina Cranesbill
Hop Clover
Mouse-ear Hawkweed

King Devil
Blackberry

SUMMER

Smooth Hawk's-beard
Great Laurel
Daisy Fleabane
English Plantain
Cat's-ear
Yellow Wood Sorrel
Deptford Pink

Asiatic Dayflower
Queen Anne's Lace
Horse-nettle
Yarrow
Hedge Bindweed
Pigeonberry
Sweet Joe-pye-weed
Hollow Joe-pye-weed

FALL

Horse-nettle
Hedge Bindweed
Virgin's Bower
Heal-all
Hollow Joe-pye-weed
White-flowered Asters
Maryland Golden
    Aster
Goldenrods
Blue-flowered Asters

Glossary

Alluvial: Composed of, or found in, clay, sand, silt, gravel, or similar material deposited by running water.

Annual: Life cycle completed in one year or one season.

Anther: The pollen-bearing portion of the plant.

Axil: The angle between any two organs or structures, as the leaf and the stem.

Basal: Situated at the base.

Beak: A long, prominent, and relatively thickened point, as resembling a bird's beak.

Beard: A group of bristle-like hairs, usually pertaining to a zone of bristles in or on the flower's corolla.

Bract: A reduced leaf, particularly one at the base of a flower.

Calyx: The outer, usually green, leaf-like envelope of the flower.

Clasping: Having the base partly or wholly surrounding another structure, as a leaf clasping a stem.

Colony: A stand, group, or population of plants of one species.

Cone: A solid mass or aggregation tapering from a circular base.

Corolla: The showy, inner portion of the floral envelope.

Crest: An elevated ridge or appendage on the surface of an organ or structure.

Disk: A round or button-like floral center composed of tiny, tubular flowers, usually surrounded by a circle of petals.

Elliptic: Being narrowed or relatively rounded at the ends, with the widest part at or near the middle.

Fleshy: Succulent or pulpy.

Lanceolate: Lance-shaped, much longer than wide.

Linear: Long and narrow, usually with parallel margins, like blades of grass.

Lobe: A usually rounded, marginal segment of leaf or petal.

Margin: The outer one-eighth of the flattened portion of a blade.

Obovate: Ovate but with the narrower end toward the base.

Ovate: With the outline like that of a hen's egg.

Palmate: Divided or ribbed in a palm-like or hand-like manner.

Panicle: An elongated or pyramid-like, loosely branched, flower cluster.

Pappus: Bristles that crown the fruit of various seed plants and function in the dispersal of the fruit.

Pinnate: Having leaflets on either side of an axis (stem), feather-like.

Pistil: The female organ of a flower comprising a swollen ovary at the base and a slender stalk (style) and a divided stigma.

Raceme: An elongated flower cluster in which individual flowers bloom on small stalks along a common, larger central stalk.

Recurved: Bent or curved downward or backward.

Reflexed: Abruptly curved downward or backward.

Rosette: An arrangement of leaves radiating from a center, usually near the base.

Scale: Any small, usually dry, and closely compressed leaves or bracts.

Sepal: A small, modified leaf near the rim of the flower, sometimes having the appearance of a petal.

Sheath: Any tubular structure surrounding an organ or part.

Shrub: A woody plant usually branching from the base with many main stems.

Spadix: An erect, fleshy spike of very small flowers.

Stamen: The flower's male organ, comprised of a slender stalk with a knob-like anther bearing the pollen.

Stigma: The tip of the pistil, often sticky.

Teeth: Marginal serrations or dentations, usually sharply pointed.

Terminal: At the tip.

Umbel: An umbrella-like flower cluster with all flower stalks radiating from a single point.

Vein: Strands of fibrous tissue in a leaf or other laminar structure.

Vine: A plant that climbs by tendrils or other means or which creeps or trails along the ground.

Whorl: Three or more leaves radiating from a single point.

Wing: A thin, membranous flap extending along a stem or stalk.

Woolly: With long, soft, and more or less matted hairs; wool-like.

Bibliography

Campbell, Carlos C., William F. Hutson, and Aaron J. Sharp. *Great Smoky Mountains Wildflowers*. Knoxville: University of Tennessee Press, 1962.

Coffey, Timothy. *The History and Folklore of North American Wildflowers*. New York: Houghton Mifflin, 1993.

Fernold, Merritt Lyndon, ed. *Gray's Manual of Botany*. New York: American Book Co., 1950.

Green, Wilhelmina F., and Hugo L. Blomquist. *Flowers of the South*. Chapel Hill: University of North Carolina Press, 1953.

Hylander, Clarence J., and Edith Farrington Johnston. *The Macmillan Wildflower Book*. New York: Macmillan, 1954.

Justice, William S., and C. Ritchie Bell. *Wildflowers of North Carolina*. Chapel Hill: University of North Carolina Press, 1968.

Krochmal, Arnold, and Connie Krochmal. *A Field Guide to Medicinal Plants*. New York: Quadrangle/New York Times Book Co., 1973.

———. *Some Useful Plants of the Blue Ridge*. Asheville, N.C.: Southeastern Forest Experiment Station, n.d.

Linn, Louis C. *Eastern North America's Wildflowers*. New York: E. P. Dutton, 1968.

Lloyd, I. V., and C. G. Lloyd. *Drugs and Medicines of North America*. 2 vols. 1884–1887. Bulletin of the Lloyd Library, No. 29. Cincinnati, 1930.

Nearing, William A., and Nancy C. Olmstead. *The Audubon Society Field Guide to North American Wildflowers*. New York: Alfred A. Knopf, 1979.

Newcomb, Lawrence. *Newcomb's Wildflower Guide*. Boston: Little, Brown, 1977.

Peterson, Roger Tory, and Margaret McKenny. *A Field Guide to the Flowers of North Eastern and North Central North America*. Boston: Houghton Mifflin, 1968.

Radford, Albert E., Harry E. Ahles, and C. Ritchie Bell. *Manual of the Vascular Flora of the Carolinas*. Chapel Hill: University of North Carolina Press, 1968.

Thoreau, Henry David. *The Journals of Henry D. Thoreau.*
14 vols. Edited by Bradford Torrey and Francis H. Allen.
1906. Reprint, 2 vols., New York: Dover, 1962.
Venning, Frank D. *A Guide to the Field Identification of
Wildflowers of North America.* New York: Golden Press,
1984.

Index of Wildflower Names

Plate numbers are shown in boldface type.

Index of Wildflower Sites

Personal Wildflower List

Species   *Location*   *Date*

_____

_____

_____

_____

_____

_____

_____

_____

_____

_____

_____

_____

_____

_____

Species	Location	Date

Species	Location	Date

Species	Location	Date

Wildflowers

of the Blue Ridge Parkway

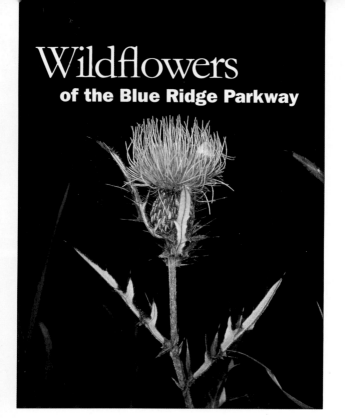

1
Bloodroot
(March–May)
p. 13

2
Wood Anemone
(March–May)
p. 13

3
Sharp-lobed
Liverleaf
(March–May)
p. 14

4
Wild Strawberry
(March–June)
p. 15

5
Giant Chickweed
(April–May)
p. 15

6
Sweet White Violet
(April–May)
p. 16

7
Cleavers
(April–May)
p. 17

8
May-apple
(April–June)
p. 17

9
Large-flowered
Trillium
(April–May)
p. 18

10
Painted Trillium
(April–May)
p. 18

11
Nodding Trillium
(April–May)
p. 19

12
Bowman's-root
(April–June)
p. 19

25
Wild Quinine
(June–August)
p. 27

26
White-flowered
Aster
(August–Frost)
p. 27

27
Dutchman's-
breeches
(April–May)
p. 28

28
Indian Pipe
(June–October)
p. 29

29
Plantain-leaved
Pussytoes
(March–June)
p. 29

30
Garlic Mustard
(April–May)
p. 30

31
Sweet Cicely
(April–May)
p. 30

32
Early Meadow Rue
(April–May)
p. 31

33
Toothwort
(April–May)
p. 31

34
Wild Stonecrop
(April–June)
p. 32

35
Speckled Wood-lily
(May–June)
p. 33

36
Umbrella-leaf
(May–June)
p. 33

37
Cow Parsnip
(May–July)
p. 34

38
Pigeonberry
(June–Frost)
p. 34

39
Queen Anne's Lace
(June–September)
p. 35

40
Poke Milkweed
(June–July)
p. 36

41
Catnip
(June–August)
p. 36

42
Yarrow
(June–September)
p. 37

43
Water Hemlock
(June–September)
p. 37

44
Flowering Spurge
(June–October)
p. 38

45
Hoary Mountain
Mint
(July–September)
p. 39

46
Bouncing Bet
(July–September)
p. 39

47
Virginia Bugleweed
(July–Frost)
p. 40

48
Pale Indian-
plantain
(June–October)
p. 40

49
*Filmy Angelica
(August–
September)
p. 41*

50
*Boneset
(August–October)
p. 42*

51
*White Snakeroot
(August–October)
p. 42*

52
*Rattlesnake-root
(August–Frost)
p. 43*

53
*Bitter Cress
(March–May)
p. 44*

54
*Shepherd's-purse
(March–June)
p. 44*

55
Smooth Rock-cress
(April–May)
p. 45

56
False Solomon's-seal
(April–June)
p. 45

57
Corn Gromwell
(April–June)
p. 46

58
White Sweet Clover
(May–September)
p. 47

59
Early Saxifrage
(March–May)
p. 47

60
Lettuce Saxifrage
(May–June)
p. 48

73
Mountain Laurel
(April–June)
p. 55

74
Blackberry
(April–June)
p. 55

75
Squaw-huckleberry
(May–June)
p. 56

76
Japanese
Honeysuckle
(May–July)
p. 57

77
Hedge Bindweed
(May–August)
p. 57

78
New Jersey Tea
(June–September)
p. 58

79
Meadow-sweet
(June–September)
p. 58

80
Virgin's Bower
(July–September)
p. 59

81
Love-vine
(August–October)
p. 60

82
Wintergreen
(September–
November)
p. 60

83
Smooth Yellow
Violet
(March–May)
p. 62

84
Halberd-leaved
Violet
(April–May)
p. 62

85
*Kidneyleaf
Buttercup
(March–June)
p. 63*

86
*Common Buttercup
(May–August)
p. 64*

87
*Yellow Star-grass
(March–June)
p. 64*

88
*Common
Cinquefoil
(April–June)
p. 65*

89
*Rough-fruited
Cinquefoil
(June–July)
p. 65*

90
*Trout Lily
(April–May)
p. 66*

91
Yellow Wood Sorrel
(May–October)
p. 67

92
Ragwort
(April–July)
p. 67

93
Hawkweed
(May–July)
p. 68

94
Cat's-ear
(May–July)
p. 69

95
Yellow Goat's-
beard
(May–July)
p. 69

96
Woodland
Sunflower
(June–August)
p. 70

103
Tall Sunflower
(July–October)
p. 74

104
Jerusalem
Artichoke
(July–October)
p. 74

105
Green-headed
Coneflower
(July–October)
p. 75

106
Wing-stem
(August–
September)
p. 76

107
Common Sneeze-
weed
(September–
October)
p. 76

108
Squaw-root
(March–June)
p. 77

109
Bellwort
(April–May)
p. 77

110
Hop Clover
(June–September)
p. 78

111
Pale Touch-me-not
(July–September)
p. 79

112
Golden Alexander
(April–May)
p. 80

113
Wild Parsnip
(June–July)
p. 80

114
Fringed Loosestrife
(June–August)
p. 81

115
Evening Primrose
(June–October)
p. 81

116
Common
St. John's-wort
(June–September)
p. 82

117
Crown-beard
(August–October)
p. 83

118
Common Winter
Cress
(April–August)
p. 83

119
Yellow Sweet
Clover
(May–October)
p. 84

120
Woolly Mullein
(June–September)
p. 84

133
Wild Bergamot
(June–September)
p. 93

134
Bull Thistle
(July–September)
p. 93

135
Field Thistle
(August–October)
p. 94

136
Common Burdock
(July–October)
p. 94

137
Lyon's Turtlehead
(July–September)
p. 95

138
Purple Dead
Nettle
(March–May)
p. 96

139
Henbit
(March–June)
p. 96

140
Honesty
(May–June)
p. 97

141
Dame's Rocket
(May–June)
p. 97

142
Goat's Rue
(May–August)
p. 98

143
Crown Vetch
(June–August)
p. 98

144
Common Milkweed
(June–August)
p. 99

145
Spreading Dogbane
(June–August)
p. 100

146
Arrow-leaved
Tearthumb
(June–Frost)
p. 100

147
Wild Basil
(July–September)
p. 101

148
New York
Ironweed
(July–September)
p. 101

149
Joe-pye-weed
(July–October)
p. 102

150
Hedge-nettle
(June–August)
p. 103

151
Hoary Tick-trefoil
(June–August)
p. 103

152
Long-bristled
Smartweed
(June–Frost)
p. 104

153
Wandlike Bush-
Clover
(August–October)
p. 105

154
Pinxter-flower
(April–May)
p. 105

155
Rhododendron
(April–July)
p. 106

156
Trailing Arbutus
(April–June)
p. 107

157
Swamp Rose
(May–July)
p. 107

158
Everlasting Pea
(May–September)
p. 108

159
Purple-flowering
Raspberry
(June–August)
p. 108

160
Common Morning
Glory
(July–September)
p. 109

161
Wild Bean
(July–September)
p. 109

162
Common Blue
Violet
(March–July)
p. 111

163
Field Pansy
(March–May)
p. 111

164
Bird's-eye Speedwell
(March–June)
p. 112

165
Periwinkle
(April–May)
p. 112

166
Bluets
(April–July)
p. 113

167
Large Houstonia
(May–July)
p. 114

168
Blue-eyed Grass
(May–July)
p. 114

181
Wild Blue Phlox
(May–July)
p. 122

182
Gill-over-the-
ground
(March–June)
p. 123

183
Lyre-leaved Sage
(April–May)
p. 123

184
Tufted Vetch
(May–July)
p. 124

185
Heal-all
(May–September)
p. 125

186
Indigo-bush
(June–August)
p. 125

187
Hyssop Skullcap
(June–July)
p. 126

188
Tall Bellflower
(June–September)
p. 127

189
Great Lobelia
(August–October)
p. 127

190
Butterfly Pea
(June–August)
p. 128

191
Flame Azalea
(May–July)
p. 129

192
Butterfly-weed
(May–August)
p. 129

205
Skunk Cabbage
(March–April)
p. 138